GUITAR TUNINGS

GUITAR TUNINGS

A Comprehensive Guide

Dick Weissman

Routledge
Taylor & Francis Group
New York   London

Routledge is an imprint of the
Taylor & Francis Group, an informa business

Routledge
Taylor & Francis Group
270 Madison Avenue
New York, NY 10016

Routledge
Taylor & Francis Group
2 Park Square
Milton Park, Abingdon
Oxon OX14 4RN

Printed in the United States of America on acid-free paper
10 9 8 7 6 5 4 3 2 1

International Standard Book Number-10: 0-415-97441-0 (Softcover)
International Standard Book Number-13: 978-0-415-97441-7 (Softcover)

Visit the Taylor & Francis Web site at
http://www.taylorandfrancis.com

and the Routledge Web site at
http://www.routledge-ny.com

Contents

Acknowledgment

I particularly wish to acknowledge the musical and editorial assistance of John Buonamassa, of Los Angeles Valley College. He realized all of the music on computer in notation and tablature, and constantly saved me from careless errors, as well as providing useful suggestions about the text. Further thanks to Richard Carlin and Larry Sandberg for helping to create order out of controlled chaos.

Introduction

Guitar Tunings: A Comprehensive Guide was written for the intermediate-level guitarist who knows a dozen or two chords and a handful of right-hand techniques. You should also be able to change chords in a song without having to hunt and peck at the strings. If you are a really advanced player, this book may cover some territory that is already familiar to you, but my goal is to offer you some new information that will expand your library of guitar techniques and even, to some extent, the way you approach the guitar.

The Perils of Standard Tuning

Why retune a guitar, anyway? If you look at the standard tuning that the guitar is played in, you will immediately notice something odd. The musical distance between the strings is not equal: From the 6th to the 5th string, the 5th to the 4th, and the 4th to the 3rd, the guitar is tuned in fourths; if you are entirely ignorant of music theory, another way of saying this is that the distance between these strings represents a distance of five frets. However, when you get to the 2nd string, everything changes. The distance between the 3rd and 2nd strings is a third, not a fourth (four frets instead of five). Going from the 2nd to the 1st string, you return to the usual pattern — once again an interval of a fourth (five frets). Because of this almost eccentric way of tuning, reading music for the guitar is a bit challenging, and many guitarists have trouble sight-reading music. That may be the explanation of the old studio musician joke: How do you get a guitar player to turn the volume down? Put a chart in front of him!

But before you assume that whoever created this tuning was brain-damaged, think about what would happen if the guitar were tuned with every string equidistant from the next one. Only two notes would have to change — the B on the 2nd string would become a C and the E on the 1st string would become an F. That would make the range of the open strings of the guitar an octave and an additional note (or a half-tone, as the case may be). However, in standard tuning, the distance between the 6th string and the 1st string is exactly two octaves. It's a practical distance, and it's easy on the ear.

Still, it makes for some real problems in reading music. Instruments like the mandolin, tenor banjo, acoustic bass, violin, and cello use equal-interval tuning, and so it is easier to read music for them. One of the strange artifacts of guitar tuning is that reading music for the guitar is so annoying that many studio musicians, having mastered the art of reading music in guitar tuning, retune their other fretted instruments to the top four strings of the guitar. They typically do this with the tenor banjo and the mandolin, which are the instruments that studio musicians are generally expected to play on movie scores or recording dates.

When you play in the various tunings in this book, you will find that the distance between the various strings differs in different tunings. That's really the whole idea — to help you to explore new harmonic possibilities. It's almost as much fun as mastering a whole new instrument.

Open Tunings or "Slack Key" Guitar

Some of the most common alternate tunings used by musicians are so-called *open tunings*. Blues guitarists have utilized open chord tunings for many years. The expression "open tuning" means that the instrument itself is tuned to a chord. There is a famous story of W.C. Handy encountering an itinerant blues guitarist at a railroad station in Mississippi just after the turn of the twentieth century. This unknown troubadour was playing a guitar with a knife held in his left hand, so there is an excellent chance he was playing in an open tuning.

Strumming across the open strings with the right hand, or with a pick, produces a chord, without the use of the left hand. Open chord tunings are very practical for slide-playing, because when a musician uses a slide or a knife, there is one less finger available on the left hand to finger individual strings. So, one reason to retune the guitar to an open chord is to simplify the left-hand fingering.

The use of a bottleneck slide or knife itself was common not only in blues but among Hawaiian musicians as well, who recorded in and toured the U.S. at about the same time the great blues musicians were utilizing these techniques. When Hawaiian musicians retune their guitars to open tunings to facilitate playing with a slide, they call this technique *slack key guitar*, because the tuning pegs (or keys) are loosened to drop the tuning of certain strings.

Small guitar, strung for Nashville high-string tuning.

There are many possibilities beyond simple open chord tunings. Any nonstandard guitar tuning is known as an *altered tuning*. When Joni Mitchell came along during the 1960s, she revolutionized the use of altered tunings. The sound of her guitar has inspired many musicians to experiment with new tunings. I use the word "altered" because, as you will see, many of her tunings were not open chord tunings but odd and interesting variations that she was able to create.

Tablature vs. Music Notation

Some guitarists prefer to read music notation, whereas others use the system called *tablature,* which has numbers representing where the player is supposed to place the left-hand fingers. For example, an F note just below middle C can be played on the 4th string at the 3rd fret, so the tablature, which has six lines, would indicate the note through the use of numbers rather than the use of notes.

Reading music notation when you use different tunings is annoying because the secret of reading music efficiently is that you don't have to stop to think about where to find a note on the fingerboard. Therefore, I prefer to read tablature in altered tunings. In case you are one of those people for whom reading music is totally effortless, I've included the music notation as well as the tablature. For those guitarists most comfortable listening and playing by ear, this book comes with a CD that offers audio examples of the exercises in this book.

In this book, the tablature reads in the same direction as the music does, meaning the bottom line is the 6th string, the top line is the 1st string, etc. The numbers to the left of the tablature are fret numbers, important to know when you play up the neck. *H* means hammering on; *P,* pull off; *sl,* slide; and *B* and *T,* brush and thumb. Usually the brush stroke plays only the top three or four strings, and the thumb plays the 4th or 3rd string. You may want to experiment by using the thumb to play a constant bass note.

Let's take a few paragraphs to define these terms for those who are not familiar with them. *Hammering on* occurs when you actually use the left hand to substitute for picking a string. Play the 3rd string open, then immediately place your second finger on the 2nd fret. The sort of "echo" note that you will hear is an A, the same note you would have played had you picked the string with your finger or a flat pick. *Pulling off* is a more aggressive technique, where you use a left-hand finger to pull the string. Place the second finger of your left hand on the 1st string at the 3rd fret. With your left-hand finger pull the string off the fret. This is little bit more difficult than hammering on, but with a little practice it isn't hard to execute. *Sliding* involves taking a note and sliding a left-hand finger to a higher position. Place the second finger of your left hand on the 1st string on the 3rd fret. Pick the 1st string with the right hand or a flat pick and then slide your left-hand finger quickly up to the 5th fret. When we use the term "musical example," it means the music appearing on the CD.

Modified Capos

One of the relatively recent developments in the use of tunings is the use of so-called partial capos. A *partial capo* is a capo that doesn't cover the whole fingerboard, but is used on anything from three to five strings. There are people who gang partial capos, with one capo covering the lower strings at one fret and another covering the higher strings at another position of the guitar. Harvey Reid pioneered the use of these devices, and they present an entirely different set of choices in terms of retuning the guitar. You aren't really retuning the guitar, rather you're tuning your ear to recognize the notes at whatever positions you have used the capo.

Nashville High-Strung Guitar

For years many Nashville sessions have utilized a rhythm guitarist who plays the guitar with the 3rd string (G) tuned to a high G. (That note is also often used on the octave 3rd string of twelve-string guitars.) The 6th, 5th, and 4th strings are also usually tuned an octave higher than usual. Roger McGuinn, the founder of the Byrds, recently designed a guitar for Martin Guitars that utilizes a variation of this tuning. This book will include a short section on high-strung guitars.

Twelve-String Guitar

For a couple of years now I have been experimenting with different tunings on a twelve-string guitar. My objective is to tune some of the strings in fourths or fifths instead of the usual octaves, and then to pick the strings individually rather than in pairs. I have included a few examples of this technique.

Using Chords with Open Strings

In the last section of this book, I will discuss still another contemporary guitar technique — playing in normal tuning but scrambling the order of notes by playing up the neck and utilizing some open strings.

Other Resources

The appendix lists some useful resources books, records, and Internet sites where you can find more tunings and information about who is using them, and even some recorded examples. There will also be some more extensive diagrams in what I believe to be the most significant altered tunings.

Because I also play the five-string banjo, I began to play in different guitar tunings almost from the moment that I first picked up the instrument. Banjo players are always retuning their instruments — it's the nature of the beast! The more you experiment with tunings, the more fascinating it becomes. After a while you'll make some choices about which tunings work best for you. Some players become so entranced with different tunings that they begin to use them exclusively or more frequently than they use standard tuning. Pierre Bensusan, a fine guitarist, plays virtually everything in the DADGAD tuning that is so common in Celtic music. Most musicians use tunings more as a sort of dessert than the main course of their meal, but in Pierre's case he became a total convert to this new style.

Many of the tunings given here are enhanced if you use your right-hand fingers instead of a pick. There are some exceptions, as you will see, but by using your right hand, you will be able to utilize the full range of all of the musical colors available to you.

Retuning the 6th String to D

The simplest and most common way of retuning the guitar is to tune the 6th string to a D note. Now play a D chord. The first thing you will notice is that you can now play the 6th string with your picking hand. Try playing a D chord in standard tuning, and play the open 6th string. To most people, it sounds terrible!

Tip

When reading the chord diagrams, note that the numbers below the diagrams indicate the left-hand fingering. When numbers appear on the left of the chord diagram, they indicate the fret number. An x means that the string should not be played with the right hand. A slash after a chord name, e.g., G ///, means that you need to play the chord four times.

D

This trick is common among classical guitarists, who tend to observe fairly rigid procedures in their approach to the guitar. Even Andres Segovia, the godfather of classical guitar, used the low D on some pieces that he played in the key of D. In addition to enabling you to play the 6th string of the instrument, you now have a note lower than what can be found in normal tuning.

Now play the G chord, as shown in the following diagram. Because you have a low D as your bass note, you don't need to finger the 6th string with the left hand.

G

Now play an A or A7 chord. You now have a choice; you can either finger the 6th string with the left hand or you can avoid playing that string with the right hand. Wherever we want you to avoid playing a string with the right hand we will place an x.

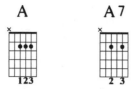

Using Different Chord Formations

Try the following variations on the chords we have already used. Notice that the D chord now has an added note, a high A (1st string, 5th fret). Adding this note is particularly interesting because you have quite a bit of musical space between the open 6th string D, and the high A.

Next try the G chord, adding an extra D note (2nd string, 3rd fret). It is the combination of the notes on the 2nd and 1st string (D and G) that give this chord its distinctive sound.

Now try the A chord, starting at the 5th fret, with the 1st string open. The notes on the 2nd string (at the 5th fret) and the 1st string (open) are the same. Because the 2nd string is a stopped note played at the 5th fret and the 1st string is an open string, even though the two notes are identical in pitch, the texture of the sound differs. It will also be very obvious if the strings aren't in tune with each other.

Tip

If you don't already have an electronic tuner, go to your local music store and buy one. Tuners are available for $20 to $30. Because you will be moving in and out of many tunings in the course of playing through the music in this book, having an electronic tuner is virtually a necessity.

As a sort of appetizer to what you will be doing further on in this book, take the A chord at the 5th fret and move it down to the 3rd fret. It is now a G chord, except that the highest note, the open 1st string, is not in the G chord but a G6 chord. It sounds really good when you move from the A, down to the G, and back to the D chord.

As you begin to get used to the sound of this G6 chord, you will start to become hooked on the sort of sounds that will appear frequently in this book.

Before we get to some actual musical examples, check out the following chords:

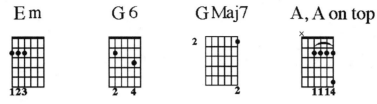

Em   G6   G Maj7   A, A on top

Our first musical example, "Windy Blues," uses all of the chords diagrammed, except for the G major 7 chord. With the right hand you can play the single notes either with the thumb or the index finger or you can alternate the two fingers. When chords are given, brush lightly across the strings with the thumb.

Example 1 "Windy Blues"

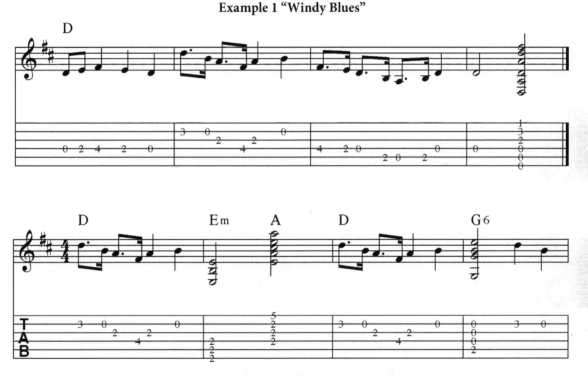

In order to play "up the neck," you will need to learn a few more chords.

First try the D major 7 chord. Notice that we have given two versions and the chord itself, followed by a variation that adds a high A note (1st string at the 5th fret).

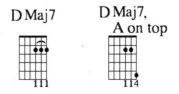

D Maj7   D Maj7, A on top

You will also need to play the G chord at the 7th fret, as shown in the following diagram. We have marked it as a GVII to indicate the fret where the chord starts.

G VII

Try to play this example freely; we have deliberately not given you the exact strings to play. Let your ear tell you what sounds good. The 7th bar consists of single-note patterns, to be played as written.

Example 2 "Up the neck"

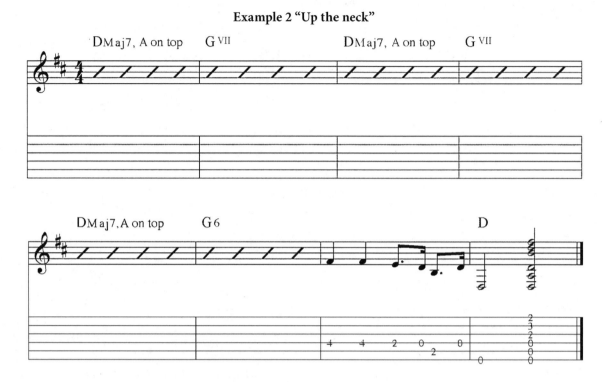

Double Dropped D Tuning

Double D tuning lowers not only the 6th string from an E to a D but also lowers the 1st string from an E to a D (the 2nd string at the 3rd fret is the same note as the open 1st string tuned to a D). In this tuning, you have two octaves of Ds, the 6th string and the 4th and 1st strings. Whereas the previous tuning produced a melodic sound and simply added an extra low note, this tuning tends to give a feeling of nervous energy with all of those pounding D notes.

Start out with the following D chords in the lower positions:

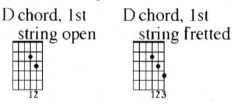

The next exercise will prepare you to play the short piece "D Demon." It utilizes these chord variations, with a couple of notes added that are neighbor notes, notes that are not in the chords but help in making the transition from one chord to the next one.

Example 3 "D Demon" (Short Version)

Memorize the phrase, and add strums as they are played on the CD.

Now that you've mastered this phrase, let's expand on it. The first note in the 10th bar is a grace note, a quick slide on the 4th string from the 2nd to the 4th fret.

Example 3a "D Demon" (Full Version)

For our final clash with "the demon," add strums as on the CD. Play freely — you're on your own!

Here's another way of handling strums in altered tunings. The first part of the tune uses only a two-finger chord, a D.

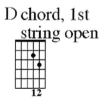

D chord, 1st
string open

Now move this chord up to the 5th fret and then to the 7th fret.

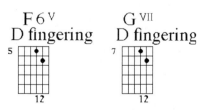

F 6 ᵛ
D fingering

G ᵛᴵᴵ
D fingering

With either the index finger of your right hand or a flat pick, play these chords in the following sequence:

D///   F///   G///   ////

Work out your own variations of how the rhythm should go. Next, make the following additions to your left-hand fingering:

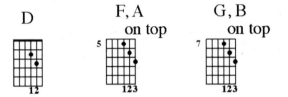

Now play the same chord sequence D F G G, but alternate between the different left-hand fingerings for the G and A chords. Next, add another left-hand finger, this time on the 4th string.

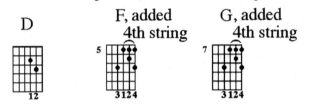

Now you have three different ways of doing the same basic thing, playing the chord progression D F G. Alternate back and forth between these three fingerings. Notice that each one sounds a bit different, but all of them "work."

Now try different rhythms for the strum, such as holding your strum for three beats as you change the chord. The rhythm now becomes: dotted half note, quarter, dotted half, quarter, dotted half quarter, dotted half, quarter.

D   DF   F   G   GG   G

You can create an endless number of variations by changing the right-hand pattern and by adding additional notes to the chord.

Tip

Stephen Stills uses this tuning on a number of his recordings — "Ohio" with Crosby, Nash, and Young and "Bluebird" with Buffalo Springfield. This tuning has a unique sort of ringing sound to the chords that can't really be obtained in standard tuning.

CHAPTER 2

G Family Tunings

Our work in double D tuning brings us to our first open chord tuning, the G tuning. The notes are:

D G D G B D

To get to this tuning from the double D tuning, all you have to do is lower the 5th string from an A to a G. To put it another way, assuming that your 6th string is already tuned to a D, the 6th string at the 5th fret will be the same note as the 5th string open.

However, if you are starting from standard tuning, you'll be doing the following:

Lower the 6th string two frets, from E to D.
Lower the 5th string two frets, from A to G.
Leave the 4th, 3rd, and 2nd strings where they are (at D, G, and B).
Lower the 1st string two frets, from E to D.

The first bit of good news is that if you strum across the strings without using any left-hand fingers, you are actually playing a G chord. Remember, in open tunings the left-hand fingerings tend to be easier than they are in standard tuning. I often have thought that beginning guitar students, especially children, who don't have large hands, should actually start by playing in the G tuning.

The second bit of good news is that the G tuning is also the most common tuning used in playing the five-string banjo. The banjo tuning uses a high G for the 5th string, but the other notes, D, G, B, and D, are identical to the notes used on the first four strings of the guitar in open G tuning. To put it another way, all of the chords you will learn in the open G tuning are also usable on the banjo.

Now let's expand our chord vocabulary, by learning the C, D7, and E minor chords.

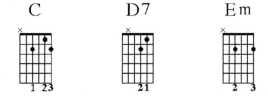

Next play C, D7, and then E minor with a simple right-hand arpeggio. The right-hand pattern is as follows:

The thumb plays the bass string.
The index finger plays the 3rd string.
The middle finger plays the 2nd string.
The ring finger plays the 1st string.

This example is in 2/4 time, playing four even eighth notes.

C/   D/   Em/   / /

Tip

You may not be accustomed to using the right-hand ring finger. This is a good place to start. Don't rest any right-hand fingers on the face of the guitar, instead keep your right hand arched.

Your next pleasant surprise will be when you play the C and D chords up the neck (use the D shown in the following diagram instead of D7). All you have to do is to play a barre, fingering all six strings with the first finger of the left hand, and you have a C chord up the neck. If you move up to the 7th fret and use the same left-hand fingering, you will have a D chord.

By simply using one finger of the left hand, you can play any major chord. For example, at the 2nd fret a barre produces an A chord, at the 4th fret a B chord, etc.

The E minor chord will require the use of more fingers.

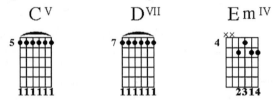

If you prefer to play the D7 chord up the neck, use the following diagram:

Continue to play the chord progression C D7 Em, substituting a D chord when you move up the neck.

You should now begin to grasp the sort of things that can be accomplished fairly easily in open chord tunings and are difficult or impossible to achieve in standard tuning.

Partial Chord Fingerings in Open Tuning

Another interesting aspect of playing in tunings is to use the open strings as part of the chord in the higher positions. Try the following chord fingerings:

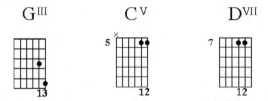

Notice that when you play the aforementioned D chord, the open 1st string is actually lower in pitch than the note on the 2nd string at the 7th fret. You are playing an F# on the 2nd string, but a D on the 1st string. Here it is in musical notation and tablature:

Example 4

Next, try the same thing, moving further up the neck. Diagrams:

G chord at the 7th fret
C chord at the 8th fret
D chord at the 10th fret with open 1st and 4th strings

As you did with the last series of examples, practice playing these chords up and down the neck.

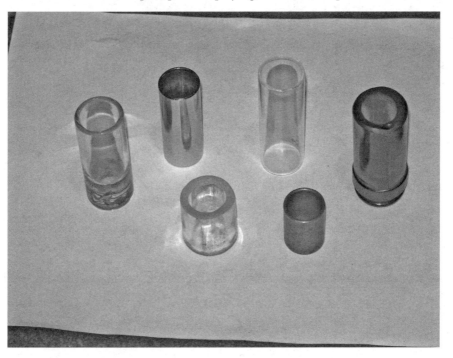

Various sizes and shapes of slides, glass and metal.

Slide Guitar

Slide guitar is one of the most popular guitar techniques used in blues playing. Various slides are used in playing slide guitars. The early blues players used knives, homemade glass slides (usually a broken soda or liquor bottle, hence the name *bottleneck*), or even a pencil. Today, there are dozens of slides available. They include glass, ceramic, and brass slides, and they come in sizes large enough to spread across the neck of the guitar or small enough to play only two or three strings of the guitar. Most of them are reasonably priced — in the range of $5 to $15. You may want to buy a couple of them with which to experiment.

Tip

When you finger the strings with a slide, you have to revise your ideas about left-hand fingering. Normally, you finger chords just behind the frets, but with a slide, in order to play in tune, you have to finger exactly over the fret. This takes a bit of getting used to, and you may find that you are playing a bit out of tune until you've mastered the use of the slide.

Most players wear the slide on the little finger of the left hand, but a few musicians prefer to use the slide on the ring finger. The advantage of wearing the slide on the little finger is that it makes it possible for you to use your other fingers as well. For now let's try some examples in which you are fingering only with the slide. (Another possibility, although I haven't seen anyone else do it, is to wear the slide on the left index finger, leaving your whole hand open to finger chords or additional notes.)

The advantages of slide-playing in open tuning should quickly become apparent to you. Remember that you can play the C chord with a barre at the 5th fret and a D chord with a barre at the 7th fret. You can also play the G chord with a barre at the 12th fret. Try the following:

Slide up to the G chord at the 12th fret.
Slide down to the D chord at the 7th fret.
Slide down to the C chord at the 5th fret.
Play the open G chord.

Each chord should be played for 1 bar. It looks like this:
G (12th fret)/D(7th fret) C (5th fret) G open

///   ///   ///   ///

Open G "Slidin'"

Here's a piece that uses the slide to play individual notes rather than chords.

Example 5 "Slidin'"

Experiment with how intense you want the notes played with the slide to be. In other words, you can either go directly to the desired note or use the slide slowly so that the listener can hear other notes along the way.

Now let's try a another piece that also uses the slide, but this time you will be playing some full chords for the first note and when you get to the D chord at the 7th fret. All the other notes should be played as single notes note chords.

Example 6 "Slidin' #2"

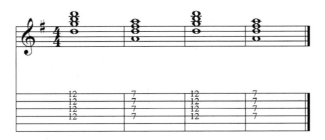

Try some of your own variations by playing different notes in the chord. For example, play the G and D chords without using the 1st string, or emphasize the bass notes.

Try fooling around with the single notes, too. With only the slightest of variations you can make your playing colorful and interesting.

Tip

Don't feel obligated to play every piece in this book exactly as it is written. The more you experiment with your own ideas about what sounds good, the closer you will be to developing your own style and even to inventing new guitar techniques.

More examples of G tuning without the slide follow.

Open G "Movin' Fast"

To play "Movin' Fast," you will need to learn the F chord. Following are three versions of the F chord in different positions of the fingerboard:

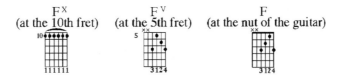

Play the chord progression G F C G. Each chord is held for four beats.

Example 7 "Movin' Fast"

G/// F/// C/// G///

Go up and down the neck, playing the chords in different positions of the fingerboard, as explained earlier. Now play the same chords, but don't finger any notes on the 1st string with your left hand. See the following diagrams, and don't use the slide for these chords. The 1st string is open for all of these chords.

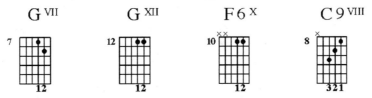

Note that the F in these fingerings, with the 1st string open, actually becomes an F6 with this fingering, and the C chord becomes a C9.

Now that you've become used to these positions, try alternating the chord shapes, playing some with the open 1st string and some without. When you use the open 1st string, don't use a slide, but when you use a chord shape that does have a note on the 1st string, use the slide. Follow the piece, which we call "Movin' Fast," on the CD. We are simply moving the chords up and down the neck.

Although the slide provides a high level of intensity to your playing, it is also possible to use open chord tunings for a much lighter, almost nostalgic feeling. The example "Roamin'" illustrates this.

"Roamin'"

You will need the following right-hand picking pattern to play Roamin':

The thumb plays the 6th or 5th string.
The thumb plays the 4th string.
The 1st finger plays the 2nd string.
The thumb plays the 6th or 5th string.
The 2nd finger plays the 1st string.
The thumb plays the 4th or 3rd string.
The index finger plays the 2nd string.

The rhythm is a quarter note followed by six eighth notes.
Add the following chords to your G tuning vocabulary:

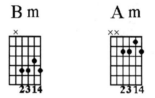

Example 8 "Roamin'"

Now try "Roamin'" using the following right-hand strum, and don't rest your right thumb on the pick guard while playing this pattern.

The thumb plays the bass note.
The index finger brushes down across the string.
The index finger brushes back up across the strings.
The thumb plays the bass note.
The index finger brushes down.
The index finger brushes back up.

Example 9

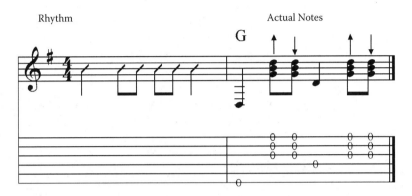

The rhythm is a quarter note, two eighth notes, quarter note, and two eighth notes.

Here's yet another right-hand picking pattern that expresses a different interpretation of the same melodic idea; again, don't rest your right thumb on the pick guard while playing this pattern.

The thumb plays the bass note (6th or 5th string).
The index finger brushes down across the strings.
The index finger brushes back up across the strings.
The thumb plays the 4th string.
The middle finger plays the 1st string.
The index finger plays the 2nd string.

The rhythm is slightly different from the last picking pattern: a quarter note, two eighths, two eighths, and a quarter.

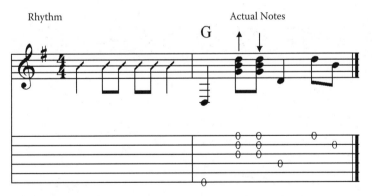

Example 10

You can also modify this strum using the same first three steps and then

The thumb plays the 4th string.
The ring finger plays the 1st string.
The middle finger plays the 2nd string.
The index finger plays the 3rd string.

The rhythm is a quarter note, two eighth notes, and then four eighth notes.

"Blues without Words"

"Blues without Words" is an extended blues solo, designed to show how the G tuning can be utilized in a variety of ways, including open string passages, pedal points (keeping a bass note the same even though the chords change), and playing up the neck with a combination of open strings and fretted notes.

For the right hand, you need to use the thumb and the index and middle fingers. The earlier blues players generally used only one finger, and this tune is playable with just one finger, but it is easier when using both fingers. Although I have provided chord symbols, much of this piece uses only two notes at a time so that playing the full chord shape isn't necessary.

The following example is actually in the key of D, even though we're using an open G tuning. It is possible to play a song in open tunings but in keys different from the open tuning itself. I haven't given a key signature because even though you are playing in the key of D, in many instances the F natural note is used instead of F#, which is part of the signature for the key of D. In playing blues, the third and seventh notes of the scale are often flatted. For the D major scale, the notes are D E F# G A B C# D, but in open tuning it is F and C that are often used instead of the F# and C# notes.

Example 11 D Scale with Blue Notes Marked

Example 12 "Blues without Words" (G Tuning)

Open G "Lonesome Blues"

"Lonesome Blues" requires that you use a basic finger picking pattern that is often referred to as *Travis picking,* after the great guitarist Merle Travis. The right-hand pattern is:

The thumb plays the 6th or 5th string.
The middle finger plays the 1st string.
The thumb plays the 4th or 3rd string.
The index finger plays the 2nd string.

The rhythm is four even eighth notes.
You will need to learn some new chords for this tune.

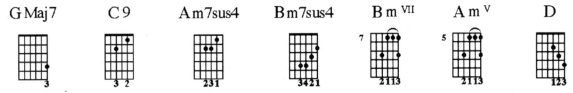

Use the right-hand pattern, and follow the chords. There is no melody.

4./4 GM7/ C9/ GM7/ C9/ GM7/C9/ G///
  GM7/C9/ GM7/C9/ Am7 sus4/Bm7 sus4/ Am7 sus4 /Bm7 sus 4/
  Am7 sus4/ Bm7 sus4 Am7 sus4/ Bm7 sus4/ D. C/ G///
  Am7 sus4/ 4 / Bm7 sus4/ D/ Bm/ Am/ /D////

One of the problems with picking patterns is that when a guitarist uses them repetitively, everything begins to sound the same, and the melody lines become subordinated to the pattern itself. To show you how to avoid this, here's another solo for "Lonesome Blues" with the picking pattern broken up. The last three bars have no melody — just play the chords.

Example 13 "Lonesome Blues #2"

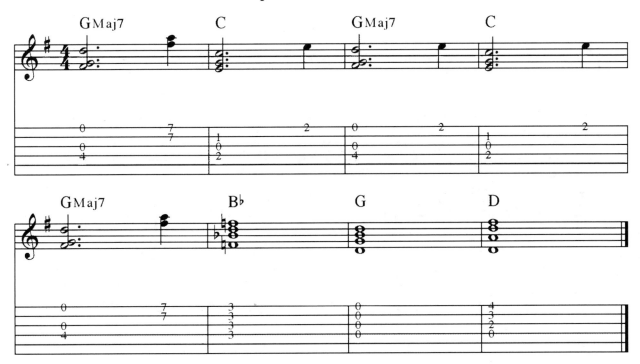

"The Parlor Pedal Point Waltz"

As we mentioned already, a pedal point is a repeated bass note that remains the same throughout a composition, even as the chords and melody change around it. At the turn of the twentieth century, young guitarists — often women — played the instrument at home to entertain themselves and their families. The front parlor was often the place where these sentimental instrumentals were played. "The Parlor Pedal Point Waltz" is in 3/4 time, and is intended to have the feel of the parlor music of around 1900. Note that in the first part of the tune you must keep using the open 4th string (D) even when the chords change. To play the harmonic at the 12th fret in bar 8, touch the string lightly with your left-hand ring finger as if you were touching it with a slide, without depressing it, and play very lightly with the first three fingers of the right hand.

Here are the chord diagrams with the D pedal points (repeated notes that have a drone-like effect). In this case the D notes, the open 4th string, are the pedal points.

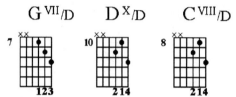

Example 14 "the Parlor Pedal Point Waltz"

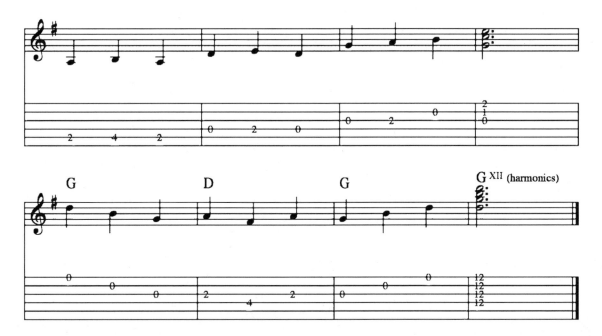

G Minor Tuning

To get into G minor tuning, from open G, lower the 2nd string from a B to a B♭ (the same note as on the 3rd string, 3rd fret). Now when you play on open strings, instead of a G major chord, you will be playing a G minor. If you're starting from standard tuning then:

Lower the 6th string two frets, from E to D.
Lower the 5th string, two frets, from A to G.
Leave the 4th and 3rd strings at D and G.
Lower the 2nd string one fret, from B to B♭.
Lower the 1st string two frets, from E to D.

When we discussed the G tuning, we mentioned that the tuning of the top (highest) four strings is identical to the tuning used on the five-string banjo. For our first tune in G minor, we will actually utilize the so-called clawhammer banjo style. To play in this style, use the following steps in the right hand:

The index finger picks down on the 1st string with the back of the fingernail.
The middle finger brushes down across the strings.
The thumb plays the 5th string.

The rhythm is a quarter note followed by two eighth notes.

It will take you some time to get used to this pattern. It is normal to have trouble picking specific strings. The initial sound you get will probably be fairly sloppy. You will also discover that if you pick down hard with your nails, they are apt to break. It takes time to develop nails hard enough to avoid wearing them down. Ken Perlman, an excellent clawhammer banjo player, sometimes uses clear stationery tape on his right-hand fingernails to protect them. Don't try to play fast until you are able to hit single notes cleanly. Be patient; after a while you will master this unusual right-hand style.

Tip

You need to have hard fingernails on the first two fingers of the right hand to play in this way. Keep your right wrist arched, and hold your right hand in a bent position.

Try practicing the strum by picking down alternately on the 3rd and 4th strings with your index finger, brushing down across the top three or four strings with the middle finger and alternately playing the 4th or 5th strings with your thumb.

Open G Minor "Minor Claws"

Try playing the tune "Minor Claws." Mirroring banjo style, it uses virtually nothing in the way of chords. Play the notes on the 3rd and 4th lines with your right index finger. We have indicated the brush and thumb notes with the letters *B* and *T*.

Example 15 "Minor Claws"

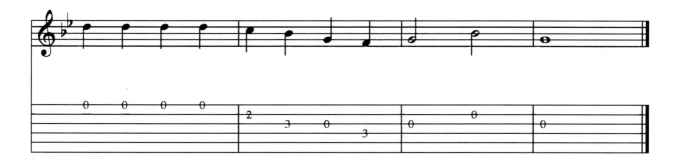

Open G Minor "Darker Than Ever"

The next piece, "Darker Than Ever," is absolutely opposite in style from "Minor Claws." This is an example of the sort of classically influenced new acoustic music that is played by various contemporary artists. Try to get as "legitimate" a sound out of the guitar as you can, by which I mean you should try to play each note as clearly as possible. Try to avoid left-hand finger noises, i.e., the squeaks, as you move from one part of the fingerboard to another.

Tip

Keep the right hand arched. Do not rest any fingers on the face of the guitar.

Playing Tips

You will need the following chords for this piece:

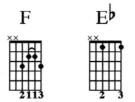

Example 16 "Darker Than Ever"

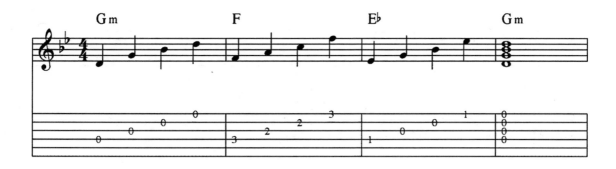

DGDGCD (Mountain Minor or Sawmill Tuning)

This is a common banjo tuning, and is used for playing a number of folk tunes, including "Shady Grove," "Pretty Polly," and "The Cuckoo." Most of the musical examples in this book are original tunes, but in this instance I decided to use the traditional song "The Cuckoo." To begin, here is the basic melody for the song with the lyrics. The instrumental solo is very much like the Clarence Ashley banjo part on his classic recording of the song. Repeat the first two lines of the song.

To get into mountain minor tuning: starting from the open G tuning, tune your 2nd string up to a C (same note as on the 3rd string at the 5th fret). If you're starting from standard tuning, then:

Lower your 6th string two frets, from E to D.
Lower your 5th string two frets, from A to G.
Leave your 4th and 3rd strings at D and G.
Raise your 2nd string one fret, from B to C.
Lower your 6th string two frets, from E to D.

"The Cuckoo"

Example 17 "The Cuckoo" (Melody)

Additional lyrics for "The Cuckoo":

Jack of diamonds, Jack of diamonds
I've known you of old
You've robbed my, poor pockets,
Of silver and gold
I've played cards in England,
And I've played cards in Spain
I'll bet you ten dollars,
I'll beat you next game.

Here is a solo for "The Cuckoo," using part of the clawhammer technique used earlier in the song "Minor Claws." The strings should be picked down, away from your body, with the first finger when playing the melody. The solo after the guitar solo uses the full clawhammer technique. You will need to learn the F6 chord. In this tuning the open G chord is a G suspended fourth (G sus4) chord. Notice that in the 3rd line, 1st bar, the 2nd string is pulled off at the 2nd fret. If you haven't done this before, you simply place one finger on the 2nd string at the 2nd fret, pick that note, and then pluck the note with your left hand, creating a sound on the open string.

Example 18 "the Cuckoo" (Guitar Solo)

The following is a solo with strums added:

CHAPTER **3**

D Family Tunings

The next series of tunings that we will play are based on the open D chord, the open D tuning D A D F# A D. Compare this to the G tuning, where we used the notes D G D G B D. Notice the difference in the distance between the strings in the following table.

Distance between D and G Tunings

Strings	G Tuning	D Tuning
6th to 5th	Fifth (seven frets)	Fourth (five frets)
5th to 4th	Fourth (five frets)	Fifth (seven frets)
4th to 3rd	Third (four frets)	Fourth (five frets)
3rd to 2nd	Minor third (three frets)	Third (four frets)
2nd to 1st	Fourth (five frets)	Minor third (three frets)

If you look at this table carefully, you will notice that the interval relationships between strings 6 through 2 in open D tuning are the same as the interval relationships between strings 5 through 1 in G tuning

Let's get into D tuning. Moving from standard tuning, do the following:

Lower the 6th string two frets, from E to D.
Keep the 5th and 4th strings at A and D.
Lower the 3rd string one fret, from G to F#.
Lower the 2nd string two frets, from B to A.
Lower the 1st string two frets, from E to D.

If you strum across the open strings, you will play a D chord, just as you produced a G chord in the G tuning strumming across the open strings. As with the G tuning, the D tuning is very well suited for playing slide guitar, and on the highest four strings it is also identical to the D tuning of the five-string banjo. Although that tuning isn't as popular with banjo players as the G tuning is, it is used reasonably often.

Here are some common chords for the D tuning:

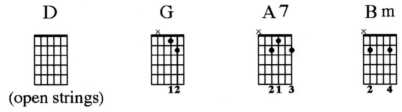

D   G   A 7   B m

(open strings)

Open D "Dreaming"

The first musical example is in 6/8 time and has a definite Irish flavor. The 6/8 time has six eighth notes for each measure of music. It is counted **1** 2 3 **4** 5 6, and felt as two beats, each of which is divided in thirds; so, for each measure of 6/8 time, you tap your foot two, not six, times. It is recommended that you play this example with a pick because there are so many single-note passages.

Example 19 "Dreaming"

This D tuning solo is intended to be a calm and peaceful musical moment. this piece. Play at a very relaxed tempo and as cleanly as possible. You will need to learn the following chords; as with the open G tuning, simply placing a barre across all the strings moves the chord up the fingerboard. Therefore, a barre at the 5th fret is a G chord and at the 7th fret, an A chord.

The GV and AVII chords are a bit of a stretch, with the little finger playing four frets above the barre. Because you are playing up the neck, where the frets are closer together, this should be doable with practice.

Play the following chords using the simple Merle Travis picking pattern that we first learned in "Lonesome Blues" which is reviewed here. A more elaborate arrangement of the same tune follows, with the picking pattern modified. The original Travis pattern we learned was:

The thumb plays the 6th or 5th string.
The middle finger plays the 1st string.
The thumb plays the 4th or 3rd string.
The index finger plays the 2nd string.

The rhythm is four even eighth notes.

G6/// A6/// G6/// A6///
G/// A6/// G6/// ////
A C# on top/// G B on top /// A C# on top G B on top ///
D/// A7 /// D/// D///

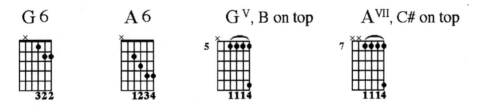

The following is a modification of the solo, which adds some interesting textures to the piece. In addition to the new chords we've just been practicing, you'll also need the following:

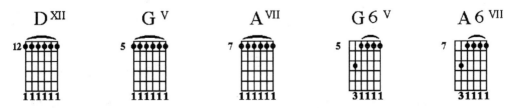

Example 20 "Dreaming" (Expanded Version)

Open D "D Blues"

"D Blues" uses the slide again, so place a slide on the little finger of your left hand. This piece alternates the use of the slide with the left-hand fingers playing the chords.

Play this 8 bar figure. When you use the slide at the 12th fret, use the vibrato in the left hand. To get the vibrato sound, slide up to the 12th fret, and then, once you're over it, make a slight wavering motion with the slide over the fret.

Example 21 "D Blues"

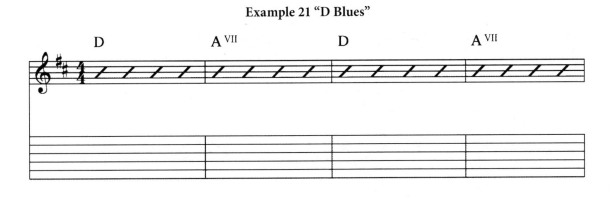

Open D "More D Blues"

Now, we are going to play the same figure but with some additional notes. This is basically the way you start to construct a new solo.

Example 22 "More D Blues"

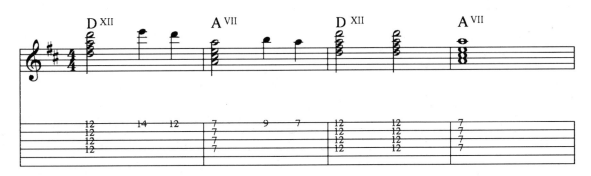

Open D "Ridge Runner Blues"

"Ridge Runner Blues" is a finger-style blues solo to be played without the slide. To play the single-note passages, alternate either the right thumb and index finger or the index and middle fingers of the right hand.

Example 23 "Ridge Runner Blues"

"Musing"

"Musing" is a fingerboard study that moves up and down the neck. You will need to learn these chords:

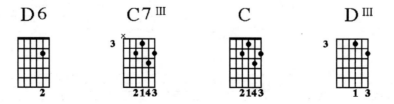

Without trying to play a specific melody, use the Travis pick from the expanded version of "Dreaming" and play the following chords:

Example 24 "Musing"

4/4   DVII /// //// CV/// ////
G/// //// D/// ////
C///   DIII ///   C /// D///

Once you feel comfortable with this sequence, try adding a few notes to the chords and experiment by adding a finger to the chord shape or by lifting a finger to expose an open string. Use your own judgment as to what notes sound good to you.

Open D "Good King Wenceslas"

Here is the melody for the Christmas carol "Good King Wenceslas."

Example 25 "Good King Wenceslas" (Melody)

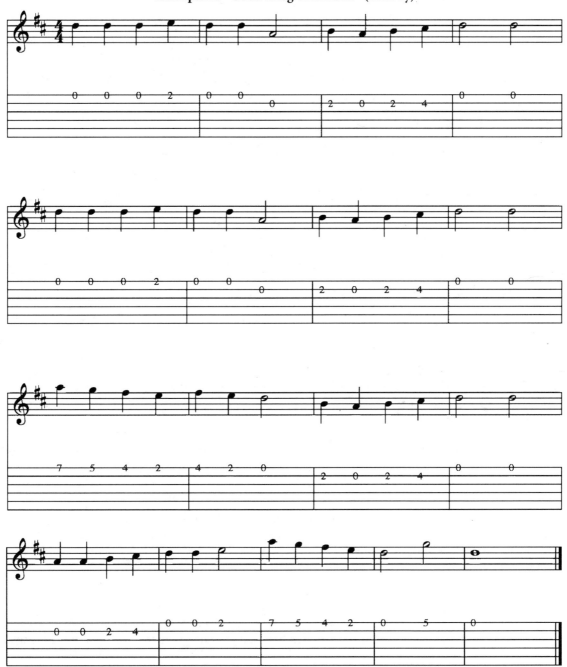

The following arrangement for "Wenceslas" is played almost entirely on the bottom four strings (6th, 5th, 4th, and 3rd strings). Once again the open tuning makes it possible to play an interesting solo that is not technically difficult.

Example 26 "Wenceslas" (Bottom Four Strings)

Notice that the solo uses the open 6th string as a drone, playing it as the first note of each bar. You can also experiment by playing the open string as a half note (twice for each bar of music) or as a quarter note. It is even more interesting to vary the use of the drone, for example, using a whole note for the first half of the solo and a half note for the second half.

Open D "In the Parlor"

In the late nineteenth and early twentieth centuries, guitar makers like Bruno, Lyons, and Healey made small-sized guitars, particularly suitable for women with small hands. A style of guitar called ": utilized the guitar to play melodic solos that capitalized on the sweet sound of these instruments. The following is a piece that tries to capture this approach to the instrument:

Example 27 "in the Parlor"

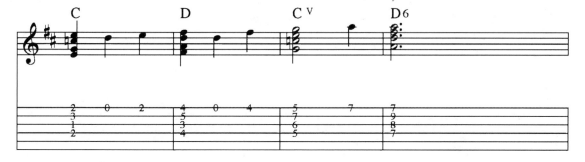

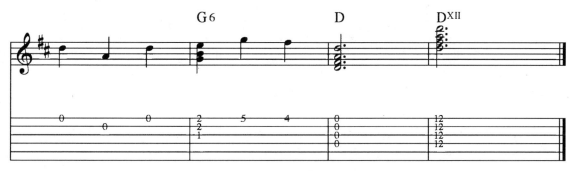

Try some variations on "In the Parlor" on different strings. For example, try this phrase on the 2nd string:

Example 27a "in the Parlor" (Variation #1)

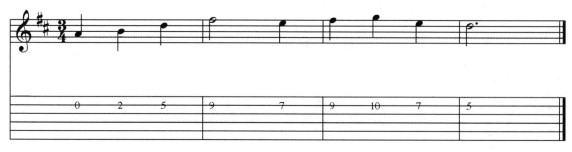

Or try the following on the 6th string. Notice the slide to the 12th fret in the 3rd bar, which simulates the sound of a bass.

Example 27b "in the Parlor" (Variation #2)

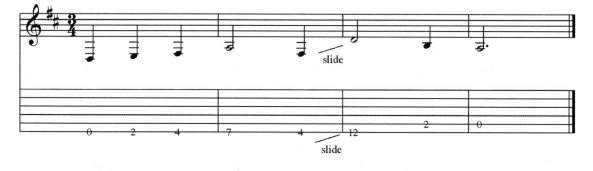

Open D "Deep Sea Blues"

"Deep Sea Blues" is another blues piece in the D tuning. This one doesn't use the slide. You can either play this solo with a flat pick or play each note by alternating the thumb and 1st finger of the right hand.

Example 28 "Deep Sea Blues"

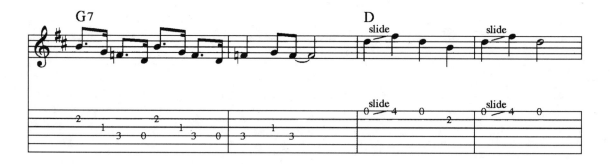

Open D "For Whom the Bell Tolls"

"For Whom the Bell Tolls" is a chord study that takes you up and down the neck. Rather than using notes, just follow the chord diagrams. The object is to get a full ringing sound that simulates the sound of church bells ringing. Play the notes of the chord together, and throw regular low-D notes, the open 6th string. Hold each chord for four beats. I have deliberately avoided naming the chords. Try to figure out what they are.

Example 29 "for Whom the Bell Tolls"

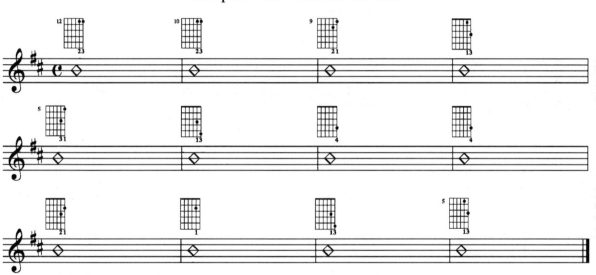

Once you feel comfortable with the chord changes, try to vary the right-hand picking style, inventing your own variations.

D Major 7 Tuning "Neil's Reverie"

The notes for this tuning are D A D F# A C#. To get there from open D, lower the 1st string one fret from D. To get there from standard tuning, do the following:

Lower the 6th string two frets, from E to D.
Keep the 5th and 4th strings at A and D.
Lower the 3rd string one fret, from G to F#.
Lower the 2nd string two frets, from B to A.
Lower the 1st string three frets, from E to C#.

Strumming across the six open strings now produces a D major 7th chord, with the major 7th, C#, at the top of the chord. Neil Young is among many artists who often use major 7th chords. There is a certain sort of melancholic indefiniteness about the chord that is attractive if you don't overuse it.

In this tuning you can play "Neil's Reverie." Here are the necessary chords:

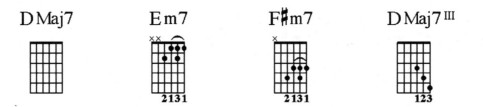

The right hand plays this pattern:

First two fingers and thumb together, half note held for two beats
Ring finger followed by the middle finger (two quarter notes)

Example 30 "Neil's Reverie"

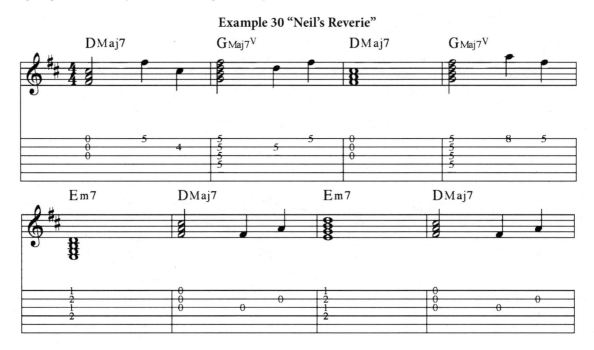

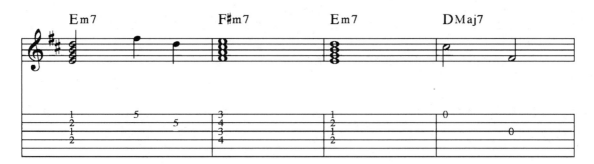

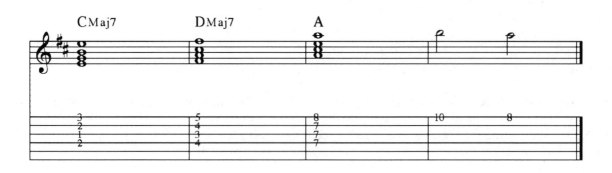

Tip

Don't feel obligated to stay with the same right-hand pattern. You can break it up into single notes played by the thumb, index, middle, and ring fingers, or you can break up the rhythm to play a rhythm as: dotted quarter note, eighth note, half note. Or you can invent other patterns of your own.

D7 Tuning "Uncertainty"

Now, from open D major 7 tuning, tune the 1st string down another half step to a C-natural (2nd string at the 3rd fret is the same note as the 1st string open). The open strings will give you a D7th chord. If you're starting from standard tuning, do the following:

Lower the 6th string two frets, from E to D.
Keep the 5th and 4th strings at A and D.
Lower the 3rd string one fret, from G to F#.
Lower the 2nd string two frets, from B to A.
Lower the 1st string four frets, from E to C.

"Uncertainty" has a dark and mysterious feel, which it never does resolve. Here's the fingering for the B minor chord. The G7 chord is just a four-string barre at the 5th fret. The rest of the piece uses open strings.

Example 31 "Uncertainty"

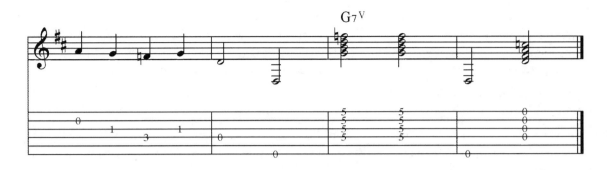

D Minor Tuning "Minor Moan"

The D minor tuning is the same as the open D tuning, except that from open D you lower the 3rd string from an F# to an F (one fret). This gives you an open D minor chord. To get there from standard tuning, do the following:

Lower the 6th string two frets, from E to D.
Keep the 5th and 4th strings at A and D.
Lower the 3rd string two frets, from G to F.
Lower the 2nd string two frets, from B to A.
Lower the 1st string two frets, from E to D.

You will notice an open circle in some of the chord diagrams. This means that the fingered note is optional: the chord name stays the same with or without that fingered note. It is up to you whether to finger those notes with the left hand or to ignore them. This technique is particularly interesting in open tunings because the tunings themselves have so many repeated notes that it creates some interesting musical textures to change one note in the chord.

Try these chords, all of which are versions of just two chords, the D minor and the C. The open strings give you a D minor chord, but notice that in the first diagram we have a fingering that also adds an A at the top of the chord.

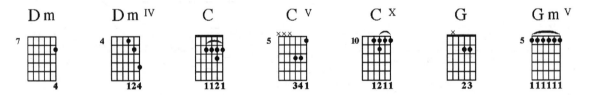

In the next piece, "Minor Moan," you will go up and down the fingerboard, but basically you will be playing two chord shapes in different positions.

Example 32 "Minor Moan"

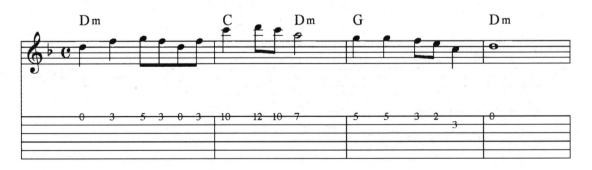

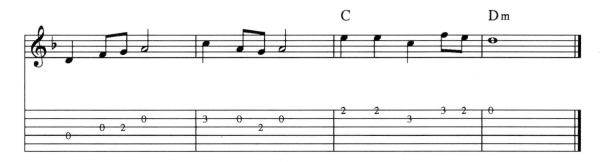

Here is a variation of "Minor Moan" that alternates between using a picking pattern and playing melody notes. For the last chord, play each note individually with your thumb, moving your thumb across all of the strings, from the 6th to the 1st.

Example 32a "Minor Moan" (Variation)

This is a very simple little piece, but by experimenting with different picking patterns, and using the different chord fingerings shown earlier, you ought to be able to come up with some interesting variations.

"Calling the Children Home"

Mississippi bluesman Skip James liked to play the blues in the D minor tuning. "Calling the Children Home," written in Skip James' style, is an example of blues playing with a gospel feel. Notice that this piece uses virtually no chords, although you will need the G minor chord for the notes on the second line.

Example 33 "Calling the Children Home"

Open E minor tuning, which contains the notes E B E G B E, has the same string relationships and chord shapes as open D minor, except that it is pitched a tone (two frets) higher. To put it another way, anything that you play in the D minor tuning can be played with the same left-hand fingerings in the E minor tuning.

D Minor 7 Tuning "Seventh Heaven"

To get to D minor 7 from open D minor, retune the 1st string from a D to a C (the 2nd string at the 3rd fret is now the same note as the open 1st string). To get there from standard tuning, do the following:

Lower the 6th string two frets, from E to D.
Keep the 5th and 4th strings at A and D.
Lower the 3rd string two frets, from G to F.
Lower the 2nd string two frets, from B to A.
Lower the 1st string four frets, from E to C.

"Seventh Heaven" is another piece that does not use chord shapes. On the fourth line of the music, in the second measure, hammer on the 1st string at the 2nd fret, moving from a C to a D note.

Example 34 "Seventh Heaven"

DADGAD Tuning

The name of this tuning is pronounced "dadgad" to rhyme with "Baghdad." We really do not know who actually created most of the altered tunings that are in common use; however, DADGAD tuning is generally credited to Davey Graham, who was the pioneer British player of new acoustic music. Davey's music went in many directions, including Arabic, blues, jazz, and Celtic music. He also has been acknowledged as a major influence by guitarists Bert Jansch and John Renbourn, whose explorations in acoustic guitar music in turn influenced numerous American players. Other new acoustic guitarists, like Martin Simpson and especially Pierre Bensusan, have developed complex musical styles in this tuning.

To get into DADGAD from open D tuning, simply tune the 3rd string up one fret from F# to G. To get there from standard tuning, do the following:

Lower the 6th string two frets, from E to D.
Keep the 5th, 4th, and 3rd strings at A, D, and G.
Lower the 2nd string two frets, from B to A.
Lower the 1st string two frets, from E to D.

With this tuning, the interval relationships are as follows:

6th to 5th string: a fourth (five frets)
4th to 3rd string: a fourth

3rd to 2nd string: a second (two frets)
2nd to 1st string: a fourth

This results in the following relationships:

The 6th string at the 7th fret has the same note as the open 5th string.
The 5th string at the 5th fret has the same note as the open 4th string.
The 4th string at the 5th fret has the same note as the open 3rd string.
The 3rd string at the 2nd fret has the same note as the open 2nd string.
The 2nd string at the 5th fret has the same note as the open 1st string.

The G note gives the tuning its distinctive qualities, which work particularly well in playing the sort of musical embellishments typically found in Irish music. It is not quite an open chord tuning but really a D tuning with a suspended fourth (the G note).

This is what gives DADGAD its slightly unresolved, almost banjo-like feel. A good deal of southern mountain music is in modes instead of keys, and the harmony is not clearly a major or a minor chord. (A mode, to give a useful, if oversimplified, explanation, is a scale that doesn't sound exactly major or minor, imparting a slightly enigmatic feel.) The major or minor note is determined by the third of the chord (the middle note of a three-note chord when counting from the lowest note up). For example, in a D chord the notes used are D, F#, and A, and F# is the third of the chord. The sound of the F# is what makes the chord major. When the third is one fret lower — in this case, an F-natural — its sound is what makes the chord minor.

DADGAD is a D-based tuning. It differs from the open D, D minor, or G chord tunings, because all of these either have a major or a minor third. Follow the music or tablature, and don't bother with chords for our DADGAD piece "Across the Mountains."

Example 35 "Across the Mountains"

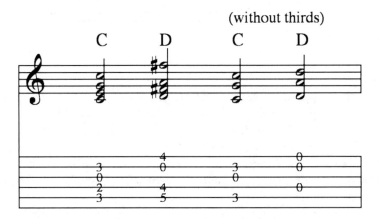

The following are the notated C and D chords, with and without thirds:

Example 36 Notated C and D chords

Because of the modal feeling in the tuning itself, the sort of embellishments typically used in Irish music fit quite well into this tuning.

DADGAD "Irnament"

Our first example, "Irnament," uses some ornaments in the 1st and 6th bars of the music, where a hammer on is quickly followed by a pull off. *Ornaments* or *embellishments* are terms used to describe brief added notes that are designed to add a bit of color to the melody. They almost always resolve into the melody notes.

Tip

Hammering on is fairly easy to master, but pulling off may require some time for you to practice before you can get a clear sound out of the note plucked with the left hand.

Example 37 "Irnament"

DADGAD "Dulcidad"

It is fairly easy to use DADGAD for simulating the sound of the mountain dulcimer. "Dulcidad" combines two right-hand techniques, both played with the use of the thumb and the right index finger without the assistance of any other fingers. The first style is clawhammer, where the index finger picks down on the strings using the nail to hit the note. We have already explored this technique with the piece "Minor Claws" in open G minor tuning. The second technique is based on playing in the Carter style. The first finger brushing down or up across the strings, generally brushing down the three or four highest strings, is indicated in the music by an arrow pointed down. Brushing back up is the opposite right-hand movement: you brush the strings back (toward your face) starting with the 1st string and ending at the 3rd or 4th string.

Note that we have written the music for clawhammer style. For the first few measures, we have also marked arrows where the BT markings are. This means that you can either use clawhammer style or the index finger to brush down and back across the strings. You can either alternate the styles when repeating the solo or mix them from one bar to another.

Tip

This second picking style is sometimes called "Carter picking" or "the Carter scratch." "Dulcidad" has no chord fingerings. Play this tune as fast as you can manage it with accuracy.

Example 38 "Dulcidad"

DADGAD "Oud Food"

Davey Graham supposedly developed the DADGAD tuning in order to play Arabic music with oud players. "Oud Food" utilizes the same combination of brushes and clawhammer playing that we used for "Dulcidad." In this case, the idea is to utilize the same notes on two different strings of the guitar, which creates a drone effect that is characteristic of Arabic music. You will also be playing a number of double-note patterns of fourths and fifths, which will also contribute to the Middle Eastern qualities of the piece. Be sure to play the opening note on the 2nd string, 5th fret. Once again, this piece requires no chord shapes.

Example 39 "Oud Food"

DADGAD "Blue Gad"

It is possible to get some interesting blues effects in DADGAD, although it's a bit unusual to use this tuning for that purpose. To play "Blue Gad," you will need the chords diagrammed as follows:

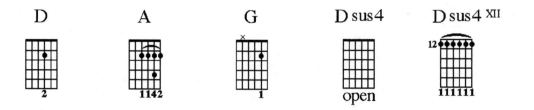

Tip

At times "Blue Gad" also uses open strings, which don't quite make up a D chord, but rather a D with a suspended fourth (G note).

Example 40 "Blue Gad"

DADGAD "Plucky Pierre"

Pierre Bensusan was one of the pioneers in taking the DADGAD tuning to a musically complex level. In the piece "Plucky Pierre," notice that there are a large number of partial chords and drone notes throughout. Where chord diagrams are given, play the chords as written. Reading the music or the tablature would be difficult, so we have chosen this form of notation.

Example 41 "Plucky Pierre"

CHAPTER **4**

C Family Tunings

The next group of tunings will center around the key of C. We'll start with the open C tuning. The notes for this tuning are C G C G C E. The low C is two whole tunes (four frets) below the standard tuning for the 6th string. The only two strings that are tuned similarly to the guitar in standard tuning are the 3rd string (G) and the 1st string (E).

Tip

If you use this tuning on a regular basis, you may want to buy a low-E string that is a medium-gauge string or at least a medium light string. This is because the low string will be difficult to keep in tune when you use this tuning.

Example 42 Notated C Tuning

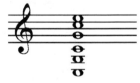

To get into this tuning from standard tuning, lower the 6th string four frets, from E to C.

The 6th string at the 7th fret is the same as the 5th string open.
The 5th string at the 5th fret is the same as the 4th string open.
The 4th string at the 7th fret is the same as the 3rd string open.
The 3rd string at the 5th fret is the same as the 2nd string open.
The 2nd string at the 4th fret is the same as the 1st string open.

The distance between the various strings is:

The 6th to 5th string is a fifth (seven frets).
The 5th to 4th string is a fourth (five frets).
The 4th to 3rd string is a fifth (seven frets).
The 3rd to 2nd string is a fourth (five frets).
The 2nd to 1st string is a third (4 frets).

Up until now, almost all of our tunings had a two-octave range, with the 1st string being two octaves higher, at the most, than the 6th string. In the C tuning, the distance between the 6th string and the 1st string is two octaves and a major third. This increased range gives the C tuning its particular unique characteristics, and enables you to play figures that seem closer to what piano players can accomplish. First off, let's learn a few chords.

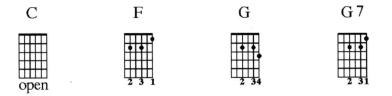

Because this is an open tuning, a barre at the 5th fret will give you an F chord, and at the 7th fret it will be a G chord.

"Impressions"

Our first open C piece is called "Impressions" and is intended to highlight some of the aforementioned features. Play this piece with as much clarity and expression as you can, and keep the tempo slow.

Example 43 "Impressions"

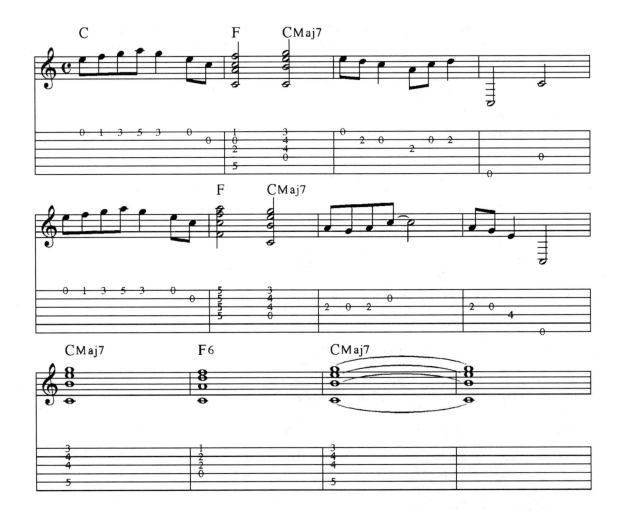

"Walkin'"

Remaining in the open C tuning, "Walkin'" explores the use of two note intervals that exploit the range of this tuning.

Example 44 "Walkin'"

Open C tuning is also a great tuning for playing slow blues, emphasizing the full range of notes available. This is a rather impressionistic sort of blues, using an odd number of bars and throwing in the B♭ chord. The B♭ chord is simply a barre at the 10th fret.

"C to Shining Sea"

Example 45 C to Shining Sea Blues

Open C Minor Tuning

Open C minor tuning is similar to open C, except that you retune the 1st string down from an E to an E♭; the 2nd string at the 3rd fret is now the same note as the open 1st string.

To get to Open C minor from standard tuning, do the following:

Lower the 6th string four frets, from E to C.
Lower the 5th string four frets, from A to G.
Lower the 4th string two frets, from D to C.
Keep the 3rd string at G.
Raise the 2nd string one fret, from B to C.
Lower the 1st string one fret, from E to E♭.

Open C Minor "Too Much Suffering"

To play "Too Much Suffering," you'll need to master these chords:

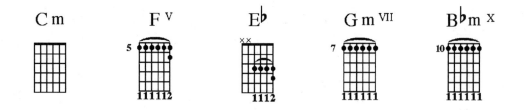

Example 46 "Too Much Suffering"

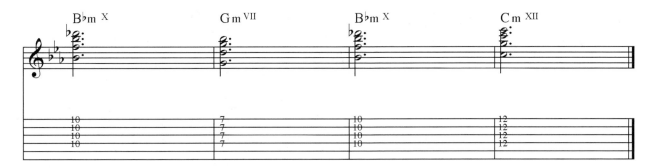

Open C Minor "Shifting Gears"

Our next piece, "Shifting Gears," adds these chords

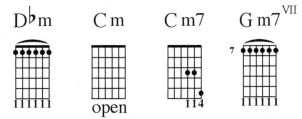

The first part of this tune is in 2/4 time — two beats to a measure, but it goes into 4/4 at bar 15. In the 5th measure of the piece there is a two-beat continuous trill on the 6th string, from the 3rd fret to the 5th fret. This is an imitation of a device that bluesman John Lee Hooker often used. Trill by hammering and pulling off in rapid succession with your index finger on the 3rd fret and your ring finger hammering and pulling on the 5th.

Example 47 "Shifting Gears"

C6 Tuning (CGCGAE)

CGCGAE gives you a C6 chord on the open strings. This tuning is called *Mauna Loa* by Hawaiian slack key guitarists. From open C tuning you will need to lower the 2nd string to an A from a C (same note as the 3rd string, 2nd fret). To get there from standard tuning, do the following:

> Lower the 6th string four frets, from E to C.
> Lower the 5th string two frets, from A to G.
> Lower the 4th string, from D to C.
> Keep the 3rd string at G.
> Lower the 2nd string two frets, from B to A.
> Keep the 1st string at E.

The result is:

> The 6th string at the 7th fret is the same as the 5th string open.
> The 5th string at the 5th fret is the same as the 4th string open.
> The 4th string at the 7th fret is the same as the 3rd string open.
> The 3rd string at the 2nd fret is the same as the 2nd string open.
> The 2nd string at the 7th fret is the same as the 1st string open.

"Marble Stairs"

"Marble Stairs" is another example of gentle parlor-style guitar. The piece has a touch of the folk standard, "Green, Green Rocky Road." To play this, you will need to learn these chords:

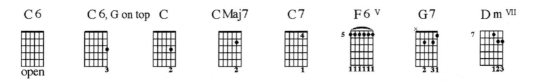

Tip

Notice how simple the chord fingerings are in the left hand. Moving from C to C major 7 to C7 to C6 only requires moving one finger.

First, try the basic melody.

Example 48 "Marble Stairs"

Next, try the finger picking arrangement of "Marble Stairs."

Example 48a "Marble Stairs" (Finger Picking Arrangement)

Double C Tuning (CGCGCD)

CGCGCD tuning is the guitar equivalent of the banjo double C tuning, which is favored by many old-time players. To get into this tuning from the open C tuning, tune the 1st string down to a D (2nd string at the 2nd fret is the same as the 1st string open). To get here from standard tuning, do the following:

Lower the 6th string four frets, from E to C.
Lower the 5th string two frets, from A to G.
Lower the 4th string two frets, from D to C.
Keep the 3rd string at G.
Raise the 2nd string one fret, from B to C.
Lower the 1st string two frets, from E to D.

The result is:

The 6th string at the 7th fret is the same as the 5th string open.
The 5th string at the 5th fret is the same as the 4th string open.
The 4th string at the 7th fret is the same as the 3rd string open.
The 3rd string at the 5th fret is the same as the 2nd string open.
The 2nd string at the 2nd fret is the same as the 1st string open.

Double C Tuning "Ren Burned" (C9)

The next example attempts to imitate the sound of the lute. English guitarist John Renbourn has written many pieces for the steel string guitar with this effect, and so we have titled this piece "Ren Burned." For the most part you won't need chords for this piece, but the following are the G and G7 chords diagrammed.

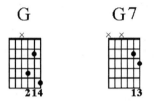

Example 49 "Ren Burned"

C9 Tuning "Banjo-It-Is"

For "Banjo-It-Is" we will go back to clawhammer banjo style, but the thumb will stay on the open 6th string as a constant drone. This is the reverse of five-string banjo playing, where the drone note is the open (high) G string. Here, the open note is the low C note.

The right-hand picking pattern is:

The index finger picks down on the strings with the fingernail.
The middle finger moves down across three or four high strings.
The thumb plays the 6th string.

The rhythm is a quarter note and two eighth notes.
There really are no chords for this piece, which is why it sounds quite similar to banjo playing.

Example 50 "Banjo-it-is"

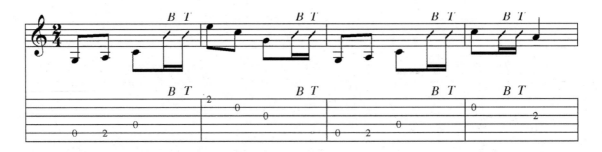

C Major 9th Tuning (CGDGBE)

From open C tuning, you'd get here by tuning the 4th string two frets from C and the 2nd string down one fret from C. To get here from standard tuning, do the following:

The 6th string at the 7th fret is the same as the 5th string open.
The 5th string at the 7th fret is the same as the 4th string open.
The 4th string at the 5th fret is the same as the 3rd string open.
The 3rd string at the 4th fret is the same as the 2nd string open.
The 2nd string at the 5th fret is the same as the 1st string open.

Our first example again has no notation, but will take you through these chords:

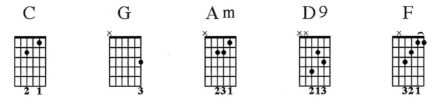

Play this picking pattern:

The thumb plucks the bass string (vary the string — 6th, 5th, or 4th).
The index finger plucks the 3rd string.
The middle finger plucks the 2nd string.
The ring finger plucks the 1st string.

Now that you're familiar with the picking pattern and the chord shapes, try this progression:

Example 51 Major 9 Tuning, Chord Progression

2/4 C / G Am D 9 using the following chords:

```
C /   G/ Am /  D9
Am/  G/  F   / //
C /   G/ Am /  D9/
D9/   //  G  / //
```

Quadruple C Tuning (CGCGCC)

This tuning is especially suitable for playing music with an Arabic or Middle Eastern flavor. There are four C notes in the tunings, with the 1st and 2nd strings tuned to the same pitch. From open C tuning, lower the 1st string four frets to C. From standard tuning, do the following:

Lower the 6th string four frets, from E to C.
Lower the 5th string two frets, from A to G.
Lower the 4th string two frets, from D to C.
Keep the 3rd string at G.
Raise the 2nd string one fret, from to C.
Lower the 1st string four frets, from E to C.

The equivalents are:

The 6th string at the 7th fret is the same as the 5th string open.
The 5th string at the 5th fret is the same as the 4th string open.
The 4th string at the 7th fret is the same as the 3rd string open.
The 3rd string at the 5th fret is the same as the 2nd string open.
The 2nd string open is the same as the 1st string open.

"West of East"

To play our example, "West of East," strum with the index finger or use a flat pick, following this pattern:

1. Single note.
2. Brush down with the index finger or the pick.
3. Brush back up with the index finger or the pick.

(Repeat all three steps.)
The *Rhythm* is a quarter note, two eighth notes, quarter note, and two eighth notes.

Tip

If you want to imitate the sound of an oud or a sitar, you may want to use a slide worn on the little finger. Because there are virtually no chords for this piece, the slide won't interfere with your left-hand fingerings.

You will need to play the B♭, C, and G chords diagrammed as follows:

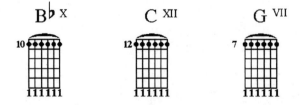

Note that you can also play the C chord as an open string chord. For the last line of the piece, play any single notes freely that sound good to you in the context of the piece. Have fun!

Example 52 "West of East"

CHAPTER 5

Other Tunings

We will explore tunings further in this chapter, beginning with our last open tuning and then turning to special tunings that do not produce an open chord (and therefore require fingering with the left hand to play the chords).

Open A Tuning (E A C# E a E)

This tuning comes from the playing of my friend Larry Sandberg, who is the author of *Acoustic Guitar Styles*, another volume in this series published by Routledge. To get into this tuning from standard tuning, do the following:

Keep the 5th and 6th strings at E and A.
Lower the 4th string one fret, from D to C#.
Lower the 3rd string three frets, from G to E.
Lower the 2nd string two frets, from B to A.
Keep the 1st string at E.

This results in these string relationships:

The 6th string at the 5th fret is the same as 5th string open.
The 5th string at the 4th fret is the same as 4th string open.
The 4th string at the 3rd fret is the same as the 3rd string open.
The 3rd string at the 5th fret is the same as the 2nd string open.
The 2nd string at the 7th fret is the same as the 1st string open.

If you look at this tuning, you will notice that, in terms of the intervals between strings, it is quite different from the open D and G tunings. In the A tuning there is only one interval of a fifth, and unlike the other open tunings, it occurs on the highest strings of the guitar.

"John Henry's Train Time" combines a bit of the melody of John Henry and some typical guitar simulations of the sound of trains. You will need the following chords:

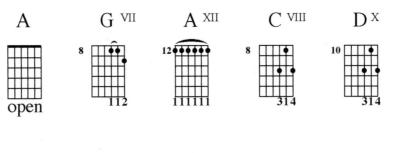

Tip

Remember that a barre across the six strings will produce a D chord at the 5th fret and an E chord at the 7th fret.

Example 53 "John Henry's Train Time"

Non-open Chord Tunings

The remaining tunes that we will cover in this chapter are not open tunings. In other words, they all require some left-hand fingering. You are probably wondering why you should bother with learning alternate tunings, which may present as many left-hand challenges as standard tuning does. The answer to that question is that the ease of playing with the left hand is only one of the reasons for playing in new tunings. The other more important reason is to experiment with interesting musical textures that can't be obtained in standard tuning or require difficult fingerings.

Our first offering is not quite a G tuning, but doesn't use standard tuning either. It is a G6 tuning, where the top four strings are in standard tuning and the 6th and 5th strings are each lowered a whole tone (two frets). The notes are D G D G B E. The string equivalents are:

The 6th string at the 5th fret is the same as the 5th string open.
The 5th string at the 7th fret is the same as the 4th string open.
The 4th string at the 5th fret is the same as the 3rd string open.
The 3rd string at the 4th fret is the same as the 2nd string open.
The 2nd string at the 5th fret is the same as the 1st string open.

You will need these chords:

G	D7	C	C6^{V}	D7^{VII}, D on top

Example 54 "Carl's Carousel"

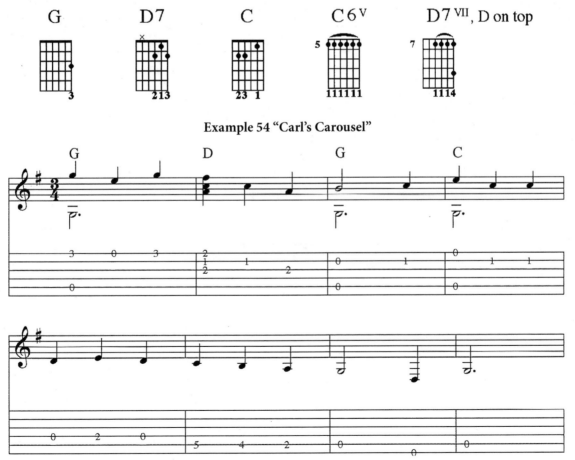

Fourths Tuning

Early on in this book we discussed the fact that reading music for guitar is a bit clumsy because of the tuning of the 2nd string. It is possible to retune the guitar to equal intervals by retuning the 2nd string up to a C and the 1st string from an E up to an F. The notes are now: E A D G C F.

Example 55 Fourths Tuning (E A D G C F)

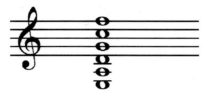

The string equivalents are now identical: any string at the 5th fret is equal to the next higher string played open. Fourths tend to produce a hollow sort of sound that conveys something of the feel of Chinese music. Notice that there are no chord fingerings for "Beijing Knights." The entire piece utilizes intervals of a fourth.

Example 55a "Beijing Knights"

"Joni's Devlish Dance" is a dissonant piece that was inspired by some of Joni Mitchell's tuning innovations.

Example 56 "Joni's Devlish Dance"

Lute Tuning

Classical guitars do not use many alternate tunings. One that they do use is to lower the 6th string to a D, the first tuning in this book. The other tuning that is used relates to the use of the lute in Renaissance music. In this tuning, the 3rd string is tuned down from a G to an F#. In other words, the 4th string at the 4th fret is the same as the open 3rd string. Otherwise, you remain in standard tuning. The only new equivalent note is that the 4th string at the 4th fret is the same note as the 3rd string open.

Very few folk or acoustic players utilize this tuning. John Renbourn is the exception to this rule. Renbourn plays a wide variety of music, ranging from Renaissance music to blues, jazz, and new acoustic compositions of his own. He likes to use lute tuning when he plays lute pieces or his own pieces written in that style. "Lute-ing" is a piece that is based on classical guitar style, and doesn't utilize any chords.

Example 57 "Lute-ing"

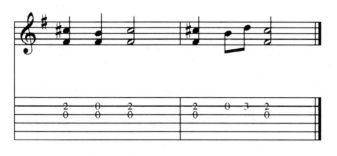

Tip

To simulate the sound of the lute, play away from the sound hole of the guitar, near the bridge. Now modify the lute tuning by tuning the 6th string to a D. The 6th string at the 7th fret is the same as the 5th string open when playing "John's Lute Fisk." The guitar is now tuned D A D F# B E.

Once again, play away from the fingerboard, near the bridge. In the last line, the same figure is repeated eight times. Make a gradual retard — each bar should be played slower than the last one.

Example 58 "John's Lute Fisk"

Duplicate Tunings

If you buy some of the tuning guides that are currently on the market, you will find that the number of tunings promised on the books' covers (e.g., "Over 500 tunings!") can be a bit misleading. Many of the tunings listed use exactly the same intervals. For example, the open D tuning D F# A D F# A D uses the same intervals as the open E tuning E G# B E G# B E does.

The left-hand fingerings are identical, so I don't see these tunings as separate tunings. Why even bother mentioning them? There are several reasons to do so: For one thing, if you or someone else is singing a song, E may be a better key than D for the singer. On the other hand, when you use the D tuning and place a capo on the 2nd fret, you will be in the key of E.

There are subtle differences between playing with and without a capo. A lot depends on whether you believe the sound of ringing open strings is desirable or not for a particular piece of music. If you do, then it is best not to use a capo. On the other hand, if you are playing with other musicians, and want a more controlled sound, you may prefer to use the capo.

Tip

If you are a performer, you need to be aware that whenever you use a capo you should expect to do a bit of retuning. Because getting into the tuning in the first place will require a bit of patience from your audience, an additional delay to tune after you have put on the capo may try its patience.

D minor tuning becomes E minor in the same way described earlier: you simply go from D A D F A D to E B E G B E.

The Same Intervals in a Tuning

It is possible to create a different sound in a particular open tuning by staying within the notes of the chord but retuning a particular string to another note in the chord. This is because it's sometimes possible for more than one chord to be available on a given string. For example, this can be done in open G tuning. The notes of a G chord are G, B, and D. Open G tuning is presented at the beginning of this book. The strings are tuned D G D G B D. The 5th string is tuned to G, two frets down from the A note in standard tuning. However, it is possible instead to tune the 5th string up to a B. By retuning the 5th string to a B, you now have the notes you still have a G chord, but it consists of the notes D B D G B D. Or, you could take another approach and tune G B D G B D. In fact, this is the way the lap-style Dobro is tuned in bluegrass.

Notice the way the intervals between the strings change in each of these tunings. The original open G, D G B G B D, is based on these intervals:

fifth fourth fourth third minor-third

When we retune the 5th string to a B, the interval between the 6th and 5th string becomes a sixth, and the interval between the 5th and 4th strings becomes a minor third. In the second variation on G tuning, the interval between the 6th and 5th string is a third, and the interval between the 5th and 4th string is a minor third. These are subtle changes, because in any of these three tunings you are still playing an open G chord without fretting any strings.

Here are two musical examples, one in each tuning. We'll call the first variation "G1" and the second "G2" for convenience. Remember that in G1 we'll be tuning up the 5th string by two frets, whereas in G2 we'll be tuning up both the 5th and 6th strings. Be aware that there is some danger of string breakage and also of undue tension on the guitar itself. You might want to substitute lighter-gauge strings to compensate for this effect. Most strings have a number that indicates the string gauge. For example, a light-gauge 1st string is usually in the 0.010 to 0.012 range. If you find that tuning a string up makes it break, simply substitute a lighter-gauge string for the one you are currently using.

To get to G1 tuning from open G, you simply tune the 5th string from a G up to a B. The 6th string at the 9th fret now has the same note as the 5th string open. To get to G1 from standard tuning, do the following:

Lower the 6th string two frets, from E to D.
Raise the 5th string two frets, from A to B.
Keep the 4th, 3rd, and 2nd strings at D, G, and B.
Lower the 1st string two frets, from E to D.

You will need the D7/C chord for the piece "Too Much Candy," which has touches of the Mississippi John Hurt piece "Candyman."

D7/C

1 32

Example 59 "Too Much Candy"

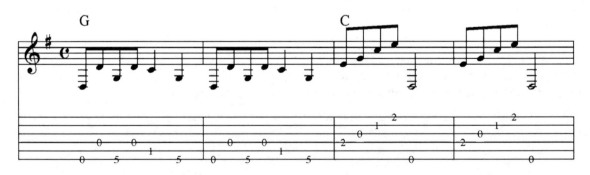

To get to the G2 tuning from open G, tune the 6th string up to a G and the 5th string up to a B. The 6th string is an octave below the 3rd string, and at the 4th fret it is now the same note as the 4th string open. To get to G2 from standard tuning, do the following:

Raise the 6th string three frets, from E to G.
Raise the 5th string two frets, from A to B.
Keep the 4th, 3rd, and 2nd strings at D, G, and B.
Lower the 1st string two frets, from E to D.

The distinctive feature of this tuning is that you have eliminated the usual deep bass sound of the 6th string.

Try playing the musical example "Turning Still." Remember that CV is a barre of the first four strings at the 5th fret and that DVII is a barre at the 7th fret. The following are the necessary chord diagrams:

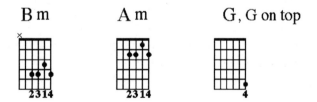

Example 60 "Turning Still"

Nashville High-String Tunings

These tunings require that you substitute a very-light-gauge string for some of the strings in standard tuning. For our first tuning, retune the 3rd string to a high G, an octave higher than the 3rd string is usually tuned.

If you don't have a tuner, the 1st string at the 3rd fret will have the same note as the 3rd string open. You can use a very-light-gauge 1st string, which will go up to that pitch without breaking. The chord shapes used for this tuning are the same ones used for standard tuning. Recently, Roger McGuinn, the leader of the famous folk rock group The Byrds, designed a guitar intended to be used in that tuning. His guitar has seven strings, with both the normal 3rd (G) string and an octave (high-G) string.

Example 61 Notated Standard and High-G Tunings

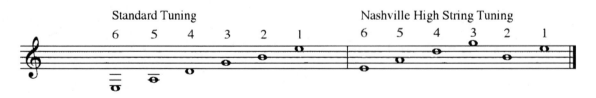

The chords used for this tuning are the same ones used for standard tuning, but when you play the 3rd string, you will be playing an octave higher than usual. To play "Country Fried" you don't need many chords. Rather than using chord diagrams for the few chords here, read the music or the tablature.

Example 62 "Country Fried"

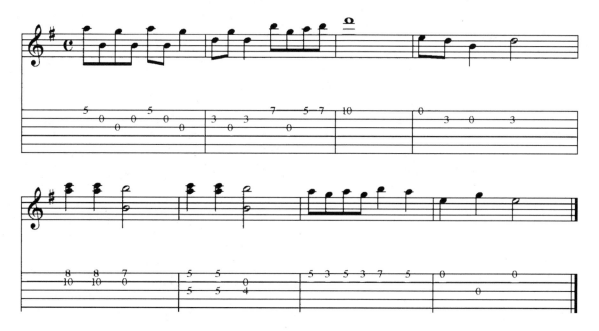

The next example requires the Nashville high-string tuning on the bottom four strings. The 6th, 5th, 4th, and 3rd strings are all tuned an octave higher than usual.

High-string tuning is often used on Nashville record dates along with a guitar in standard tuning. This provides an interesting "doubling" effect, such as using a twelve-string guitar but with a less clunky sound and a much greater ease of playing. Paul Simon has often used a high-strung guitar on his recordings.

Here is a series of chords for our next piece. The chords on a high-strung guitar should be played as written.

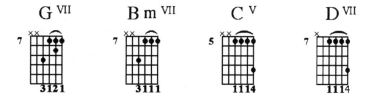

Play each chord for four beats. Try the following progression in the same way, four beats to a chord. This progression played both in standard and high-strung tunings also appears on the CD.

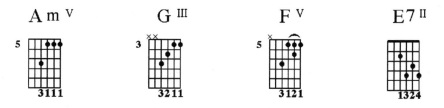

The next example, "Leadbelly's Music Box," is inspired by the folk blues guitarist Huddie Ledbetter, who was also known as Leadbelly. Leadbelly often started songs on the I7 chord rather than the I chord (A7 in the key of A, rather than A). So "Leadbelly's Music Box" begins with an A7th chord. You will need the following right-hand strum for "Leadbelly's Music Box":

The thumb plays the 6th or 5th string.
The thumb plays the 4th string.
The index finger plays the 2nd string.
The thumb plays the 6th or 5th string.
The middle finger plays the 1st string.
The thumb plays the 4th string.
The index finger plays the 2nd string.

The *rhythm* is a quarter note, followed by two eighth notes and then four eighth notes.

When you play the up-the-neck chords, play the open 6th or 5th strings only when they sound good. Otherwise, keep the strum pattern with your thumb on the 4th string and alternate with the 3rd. There is no melody; play the chords as written.

A7/// //// G/// ///
Em/// //// A7/// ////

Now, play the same piece with chords up the neck. Follow these chord diagrams:

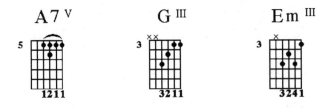

Example 63

A7V/// //// GIII/// ////
EmIII/// //// A7V/// ////

For your last go-around, move the chords up the neck as shown:

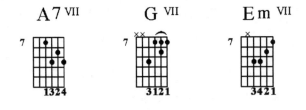

A7V/// //// GIII/// ////
EmIII/// ///// A7 V/// ////

Try experimenting with more solos using the high-strung tuning. It is a unique effect if you don't overuse it. It has the advantage of brilliant high sounds, but is really lacking in the bass register.

12 string guitar.

Twelve-String Guitar Tuning Methods

About three years ago, I decided that it might be fun to pick some of the strings of the twelve-string guitar individually rather than always playing them in pairs. This is quite a difficult task, because it is difficult to get your right-hand fingers in the narrow distance between the pairs of strings. Normally, the twelve-string guitar is tuned as:

E E A A D D G G B B E E

The 6th, 5th, 4th, and 3rd strings are usually tuned with the higher-pitched strings tuned to standard tuning and the bass strings tuned in octaves. Many players also tune the 3rd string in octaves. Some musicians tune the string closer to the face as the "low" string; other players do the reverse, with the higher string first and the lower string next. The easiest thing to do is to buy a set of strings made for the twelve-string; then you don't have to worry about whether a string will break if you tune it too high. The octave 3rd string, in particular, is easy to break, because it is actually tuned above the high E, to the note at the 1st string, 3rd fret. It used to be a real nightmare to tune the twelve-string, but with the combination of improved tuning gears and electronic tuners, it is quite a bit easier now.

Tip

Once again, if you use the capo, expect more tuning problems. Capos are difficult with the twelve-string guitar because the pressure that it takes to get the capo evenly across the neck is considerable.

Some players tune the twelve-string guitar down to make for easier left-hand fingering and to get a heavier bass sound. Typically, the people who tune it down tune everything down a tone (two frets) or a tone-and-a-half (three frets), although it is of course possible to tune it even lower if one wishes.

In the three years I have been trying to master retuning the twelve-string, what I have worked out is that I retune the 4th and 3rd strings. Instead of using octaves, I use either fourths or fifths. So, instead of D and D an octave higher, I use D and either A or G. I then tune the 3rd string in a similar way, keeping the low G but tuning the higher string to either a C or a D. Sometimes I use just fifths or fourths, sometimes I will tune one set to fifths and the other to fourths. I avoid retuning the 6th and 5th strings, because I find the booming sound doesn't highlight the change in tuning in a way that I enjoy. I haven't gotten around to retuning the 2nd and 1st strings yet.

Fifths tunings on 4th and 3rd strings are E E A A D A G D B B E E. Fourths tuning on 4th and 3rd strings are E E A A D G G C B B E E.

The tunings are notated as follows:

Example 64 Twelve-String Notation

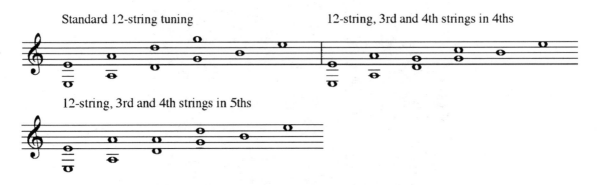

Don't get frustrated if you have trouble picking the strings separately. First, try the tuning described earlier: 6th, 5th, 2nd, and 1st strings tuned to standard tuning, the 4th string tuned either to D A or A D, and the 3rd string tuned either to G D or D G (it depends on which string you tune higher). A considerable past of the next example, "12 X 5," is played on the 4th and 3rd strings, which are tuned in fifths. Pick the note closer to your face with the right thumb and the other one with the index finger.

Example 65 "12 X 5" (EE AA DA GD BB EE)

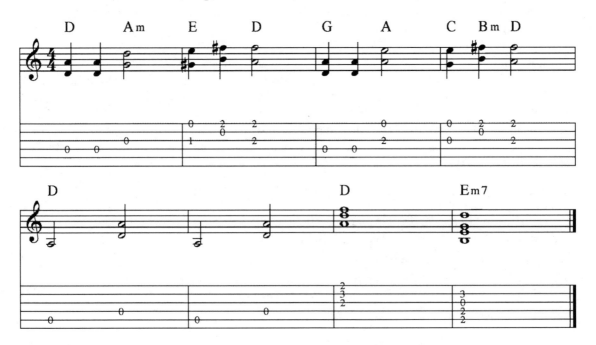

Try the same piece with a few chords thrown in where you play both pairs of strings but get different notes. Whenever you play the 4th and 3rd strings, be sure to play both the pairs in order to take advantage of this unusual tuning. You will need the following chords:

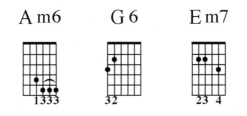

Tip

The A minor 6 is a little tricky; you need to play the top three strings with your left ring finger.

Example 66 "Openings" (EE AA DG GC BB EE)

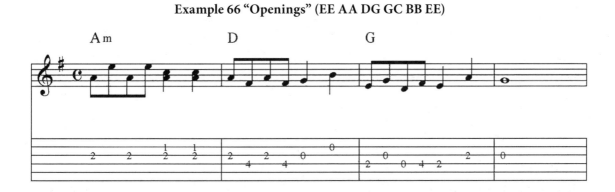

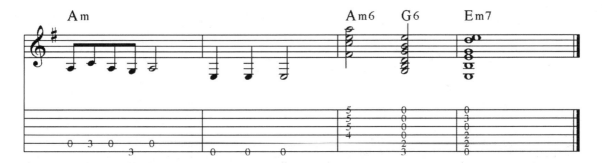

"White Men at Eagle Pass" uses the twelve-string tuning to simulate American Indian music as heard in western movies! The 4th and 3rd strings are tuned in fifths again, with D and A for the 4th string and G and D for the 2nd string. The chords are played only on the top three strings.

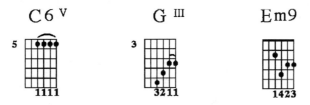

Example 67 "White Men at Eagle Pass"

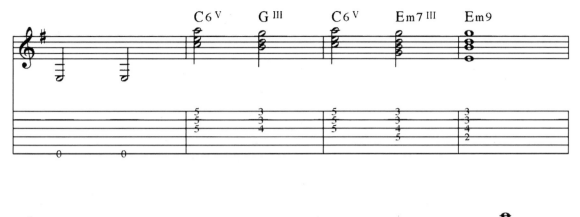

CHAPTER 6

Tricks in Standard Tuning

In this final chapter, we'll look at some other ways to create unusual tonalities on the guitar. We will focus on the use of capos and partial capos and ways to create chords in standard tunings to maximize the use of open strings.

Using Capos

The capo is generally used when a singer wants to change the key of a song without changing the left-hand fingerings. For example, if you are singing a song in the key of C, and the notes are just a little bit too low for you to sing, by placing the capo on the 1st fret of the guitar you can still use the C fingerings in the left hand, but you are actually in the key of D♭. If the key is still too low for you to sing comfortably in, you can move the capo up the neck as high as you need to go.

Musicians unfamiliar with guitarists' reliance on capos have sometimes made interesting mistakes when notating popular songs. When rock and roll and folk music first became popular in the middle and late 1950s, most of the people doing music instruction folios were piano players. They would faithfully transcribe songs by Bob Dylan, for example, in their actual pitch, calling for, e.g., a D♭ chord shape, rather than understanding that the key of D♭ was arrived at with the use of the capo. This is something you will rarely see in contemporary music folios because many of the arrangers are guitarists or are familiar with the guitar.

There is also another reason to use the capo: to increase the range of musical colors available to you. This is particularly true if you are playing in a group with at least one other guitarist. Let's say the other guitarist is playing in the key of C. To put it another way, let's say the song your band is playing is in the key of C, and the chords played are C, F, G7, and B♭. You can achieve the same sounding chords by putting your capo on the 5th fret and playing the chord shapes for G, C, D7, and F. The two guitars playing together will now sound like a small orchestra, instead of two people playing pretty much the same thing. This adds an attractive color to the playing of your band.

Some musicians use the capo because they like the sound of the guitar in the higher register. The capo will also have some other effects. Applying it will usually cause the strings to go slightly out of tune, so you will have to retune. It also will tend to cut the ringing sound of open strings, because even though you are playing on some open strings, the capo is, to some extent, muting the sound of the open strings. Depending upon your musical taste, and the particular song you are playing, this can be a good thing or a bad thing.

Harvey Reid is a guitarist who has advanced the concept of the partial capo, which he says was invented by Lyle Shabram. The capo that Reid uses is called the *third hand capo*, which can be used on some strings while leaving

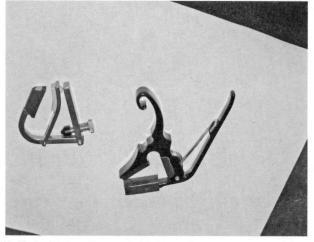

Shubb partial capo; Kyser partial capo.

Vega 1913 vintage guitar.

the others as is. This capo has six rubber discs, one for each string, and they each can be rotated so that the discs contact any or all strings. This is a very interesting concept, and is quite workable.

The only downside of the third hand capo is that adjusting the discs takes some time, and if you are not careful, it will produce a muffled sound. Consequently, several manufacturers, including Rick Shubb and Kyser, have come out with their own versions of the partial capo. The Shubb capo is screw-operated. You place it on the 5th, 4th, and 3rd strings and then tighten the attached screw. The Kyser capo is clamp-operated. Again, each system has its advantages. The Kyser's main advantage is that you can readily clamp and unclamp the capo, whereas the advantage of the Shubb capo is that, when you tighten the screw properly, it seems to provide you with a more consistent sound.

Tip

All of these devices cost about $20, so you might want to experiment with each of them or even buy a couple of them.

It is also possible to use more than one partial capo simultaneously. For example, you might place one capo on the 5th fret, covering the bass strings (6th, 5th, and 4th), and the other one on the 7th fret, covering the treble strings (3rd, 2nd, and 1st). Partial capos are particularly useful when you use alternative tunings, as you will shortly see.

Using the Partial Capo

The following are the notes of the guitar in standard tuning:

Example 68 Standard Tuning

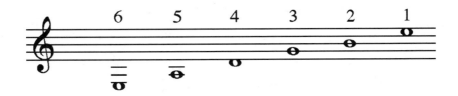

From standard tuning, tune your 6th and 1st strings down two frets from E to D and the 3rd string down one fret to an F#. The string equivalents are:

The 6th string is an octave lower than the 4th string.
The 5th string at the 5th fret has the same note as the 4th string open.
The 4th string at the 4th fret has the same note as the 3rd string open.
The 3rd string at the 5th fret has the same note as the 2nd string open.
The 2nd string at the 3rd fret has the same note as the 1st string open.

The actual notes of the guitar are now:

The 6th string is a D.
The 5th string is a D an octave lower.
The 4th string is a G.
The 3rd string is a B.
The 2nd string is an A.
The 1st string is a D.

Now place the partial capo on the 5th fret; in this case, I am using the Shubb capo to cover the 5th, 4th, and 3rd strings. The notes are as follows:

Example 68a with Partial Capo at the 5th Fret

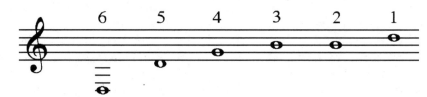

The 6th string is a D.
The 5th string is a D an octave higher.
The 4th string is a G.
The 3rd string is a B.
The 2nd string is a B (the 3rd and 2nd strings are the same note).
The 1st string is a D.

With the partial capo at the 5th fret, the notes are as follows:

Example 68b Tuning with the Partial Capo at the 5th Fret

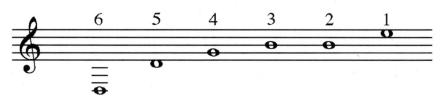

"Partial Fulfillment"

We will use this tuning to play "Partial Fulfillment." You will need to learn these chords:

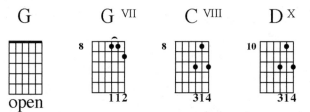

Example 69 "Partial Fulfillment"

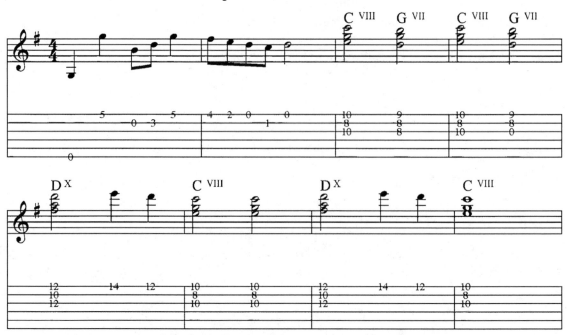

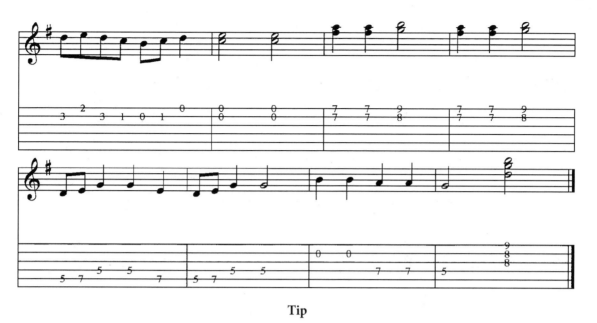

Tip

Remember that the 1st, 2nd, and 6th strings are open, so the notes in the first two bars of line three are played at the nut of the guitar, below which the capo is placed.

"Country Rhodes"

"Country Rhodes," the next partial capo example, covers the 6th, 5th, and 4th strings at the 5th fret (I am using the Kyser clamp capo for this one on the CD). Before you place the capo, tune the 6th string down two frets from standard tuning, so your notes from the 6th to 1st string are: D A D G B D.

Example 70

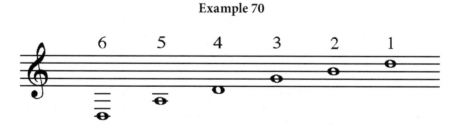

With the partial capo at the 5th fret, the notes become: D D G C B D.

Example 70a

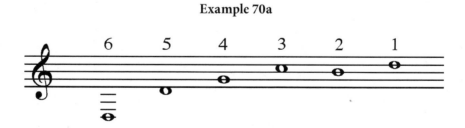

You will need to learn these chords for "Country Rhodes":

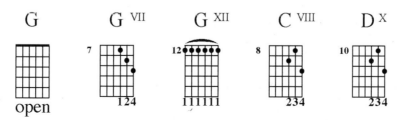

Example 71 "Country Rhodes"

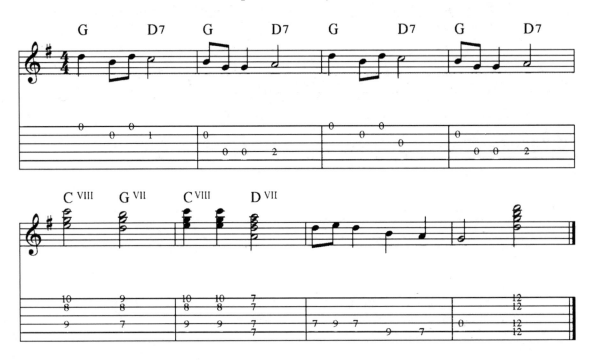

"Nine Frets High"

"Nine Frets High" is played with the Shubb capo at the 9th fret. Before you use the capo, you need to retune the guitar to D A C G A D.

Example 72 before Using the Capo

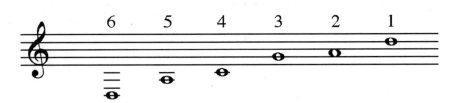

Starting from standard tuning:

Lower the 6th string two frets, from E to D.
Keep the 5th string at A.
Lower the 4th string two frets, from D to C.
Keep the 3rd string at G.
Lower the 2nd string two frets, from B to A.
Lower the 1st string two frets, from E to D.

The string equivalents are:

The 6th string at the 7th fret has the same note as the 5th string open.
The 5th string at the 3rd fret has the same as the 4th string open.
The 4th string at the 7th fret has the same as the 3rd string open.
The 3rd string at the 2nd fret has the same as the 2nd string open.
The 2nd string at the 5th fret has the same as the 1st string open.

With the capo on at the 9th fret, covering the 5th, 4th, and 3rd strings, the notes of the guitar are now: D F# A E A D.

Example 73 with the Partial Capo at the 9th Fret

Notice that with the capo this high up the neck, the 4th string is actually higher than the 2nd string. The 2nd string open now has the same pitch as the 4th string with the capo on.

Example 74 "Nine Frets High"

This is just the tip of the iceberg when it comes to using partial capos. My intention is to get you started on combining the use of the partial capo with open tunings. Harvey Reid's book on the use of partial capos is listed in the Bibliography, and is a useful resource.

Open String Chords in Standard Tuning

The following few pages are devoted to using standard tuning but involve playing of chords in different positions of the neck that utilize open strings. This simulates the effects obtained by using open tunings but can be done while staying in standard tuning. The key to playing these chords is observing which strings can be played open. Be careful to avoid the strings marked with an x, which do not sound good with the rest of the chord.

"Many Openings"

For the tune "Many Openings," you will need the following chords. Just play a single-note arpeggio — right thumb, index, middle, and ring fingers.

Example 75 "Many Openings"

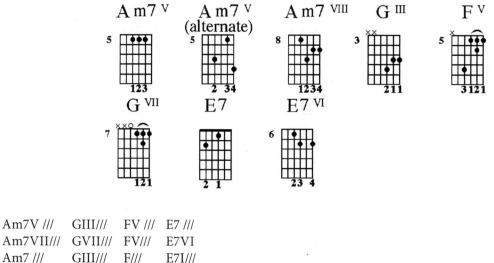

Am7V ///   GIII///   FV ///   E7 ///
Am7VII///   GVII///   FV///   E7VI
Am7 ///   GIII///   F///   E7I///

Each chord gets four beats. On the last line where there is no fret indicator, play the chord at the 1st and 2nd frets.

"Opening the E Blues"

For "Opening the E Blues," we will use the same principles as in our previous tune. This is a blues in the key of E. Once again, I haven't given you a melody here. Use a blues right-hand strum — with the thumb and index finger, or the thumb, index, and middle fingers, or you can play the chords with a flat pick.

The chord diagrams are shown for each chord. Each chord gets four beats.

Example 76 "Opening E Blues"

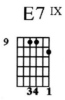

E7IX /// //// //// ////

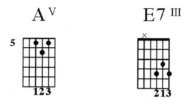

AV /// //// E7III///

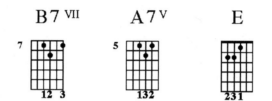

B7VII /// A7V/// E/// E ///

Off the Wall Tunings: A Brief Inventory

We have previously pointed out that any open tuning can be modified by changing one of the notes in the chord to another that is also in the chord. To refresh your memory: the open G tuning DGDGBD can be modified to DBDGBD or, for that matter, to GGDGBD or DBDGGB, and so forth. However, there are a number of other tunings that William Ackerman, Alex DeGrassi, Michael Hedges, Joni Mitchell, and others have used at various times.

Tip

Keep in mind that you can also modify these tunings by tuning all of the strings up or down, as long as you preserve the same relationships. Many of the books that promise to show you an extravagant number of tunings are simply repeating the same tunings with all of the notes raised or lowered. We have chosen not to repeat tunings that start on different notes but to use the same intervals (distance from one string to another). Also, remember that for some tunings you may want or have to change the string gauges to avoid breaking the strings.

For each of the following examples, the 6th string is the first one listed.

D7 tuning	D A D F# C D
DADGAD variation	D A D E A D
Double D, no third of the chord	D A D D A D
C6 C G C G A E	One of the many tunings used by Hawaiian slack key guitarists
Another C6	C A C G C E
D6 9	D A D F# B E
Double E, double A	E A D E A E
E minor suspended fourth	E B E G A E or lower the 1st string to a D, giving you Em7sus4 or E A D G B E
C suspended fourth	C G C G C F
A suspended fourth	D A E E A A
C major 9 suspended fourth	C D C F C E
C major 9	C G D G B E

C 6/9	C G D G A D (often used by Lawrence Juber and El McMeen)
Standard with C bass	C A D G B E
Drones	E E E E E E (6th and 5th the same, 4th and 3rd an octave higher, 2nd and 1st another octave higher)
E E B B B B	(same basic idea as the previous tuning)
B minor 9	F A D G B E, one of a number of Hawaiian slack key tunings

Here are some Joni Mitchell tunings (you can get plenty of Joni Mitchell tunings on the Internet):

C minor 7 suspended fourth	C G B♭ E F B♭
E9	E E V F# G# V
Open G	G octave lower than the 5th string, G D G B D
C7 suspended fourth	C G B♭ E F B♭

A few other tunings that I've run into along the way:

Standard, lowered E	E♭ A D B G B E
D7 suspended fourth	D A D G C C
Mostly fifths	C G D A E G

Chord Charts

The following are chords for the most common alternate tunings. I have avoided giving chords in the dropped D tunings because the chord positions are so close to standard tuning chords.

There are two exhaustive books of chords, Mark Hanson's *Complete Guide to Alternate Tunings* and Chad Johnson's *Alternate Tuning Chord Dictionary*, both listed in the Bibliography. If you get deeply involved in playing in alternate tunings, I suggest you pick up one of these books.

In the meantime, the following chord charts ought to keep you busy for some time. The chords listed are the most basic ones that will cover the majority of tunes. The tunings included are Open G, Open D, DADGAD, and Open C.

Chords in Open G Tuning (DGDGBD)

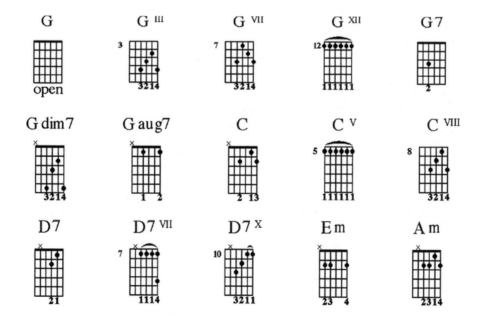

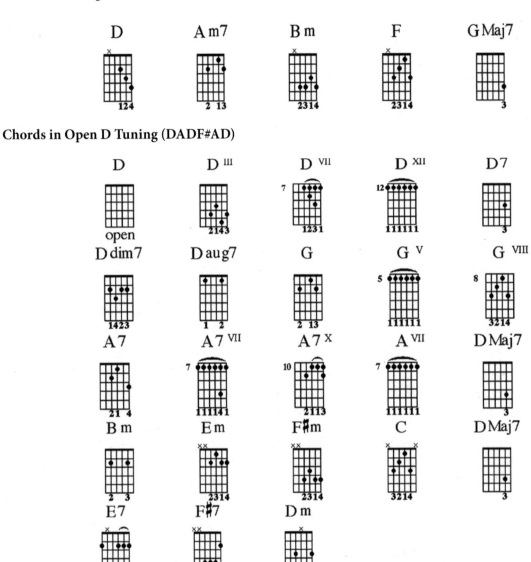

Chords in Open D Tuning (DADF#AD)

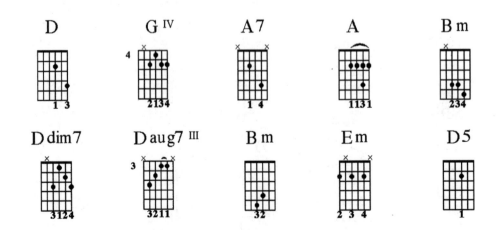

Chords in D Suspended fourth Tuning (DADGAD)

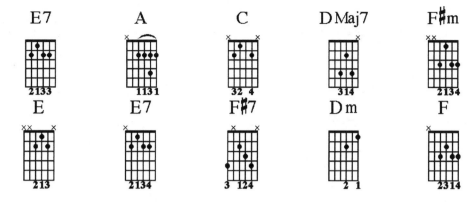

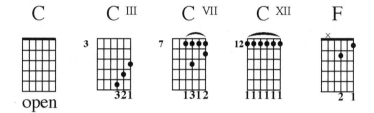

Chords from Open C Tuning (CGCGCE)

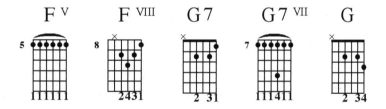

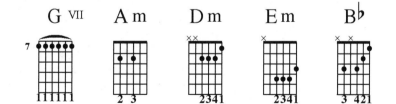

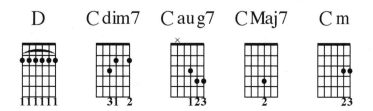

Bibliography

Dan Axelrod, *The "Axlerod Axe" System of Improvising Harmonized Leads for 12 String Guitar,* Warner Bros., Inc. (This book is so old, it comes with an LP sound sheet.)

*Tom Ball, *Dropped D Tuning for Fingerstyle Guitar,* Centerstream, distributed by Hal Leonard.

Pierre Bensusan, *The Guitar Book,* Hal Leonard.

Patrick Breen, *Bear and Fish's Pocket Guide to Alternate Tunings for Guitar,* No publisher listed.

Patrick Breen, *The Starvin' Students Alternate Tunings Workbook for Guitar,* No publisher listed.

Alex de Grassi, *Guitar Collection,* Hal Leonard.

Mark Dziuba, *Introducing Alternate Tunings,* Alfred Music.

Tommy Flint, *Country, Folk Bluegrass Guitar Tunings,* Mel Bay Publications.

Stefan Grossman, *Book of Guitar Tunings,* Amsco (Music Sales).

Stefan Grossman, *Solos in Open Tunings,* Mel Bay Publications.

*Stefan Grossman, Duck Baker, and El McMeen, *Mel Bay's Complete Celtic Fingerstyle Guitar Book,* Mel Bay Publications.

Mark Hanson, *Alternate Tunings Picture Chords,* Accent on Music, distributed by Music Sales Corp.

Mark Hanson, *The Complete Book of Alternate Tunings,* Accent on Music, distributed by Music Sales Corp.

Mark Hanson, *Masters of Hawaiian Slack Key Guitar,* Accent on Music, distributed by Music Sales Corp.

*Julie Henigan, *DADGAD Tuning,* Mel Bay Publications.

Chad Johnson, *Alternate Tuning Chord Dictionary,* Hal Leonard.

Leonard Kwan, *Slack Key Instruction Book,* Tradewinds Recording Publications.

*Paul Lolax, *Guitar Solos in Open 7 Altered Tunings,* Mel Bay Publications.

Woody Mann, *The Gig Bag Book of Alternate Tunings,* Music Sales Corp.

Ron Middlebrook, *Open Guitar Tunings,* Centerstream, distributed by Hal Leonard.

Al Petteway, *Whispering Stones,* Mel Bay Publications.

Tom Principato, *Open-String Guitar Chords,* Hal Leonard.

Harvey D. Reid, *The Third Hand Capo; A New Frontier in Guitra,* Warmwater Press.

John Renbourn, *The Nine Maidens, the Hermit, Stefan and John,* Hal Leonard.

*Jeffrey Pepper Rodgers, Ed., *Alternate Tunings Guitar Collection,* String Letter Publishing, distributed by Hal Leonard.

Martin Simpson, *Teaches Alternate Tunings* (with a DVD), Alfred Music.

Martin' Simpson, *The Acoustic Guitar of Martin Simpson,* Accent on Music, distributed by Music Sales Corp.

*Matt Smith, *Alternate Tunings Essential Skills,* Cherry Lane Music, distributed by Hal Leonard.

John Stripes and Peter Lang, *20th Century Masters of Fingerstyle Guitar,* Hal Leonard.

---

* The book comes with a CD.

David Wilcox, *The David Wilcox Collection,* Hal Leonard.
Windham Hill Guitar Sampler, Hal Leonard.

Tip

Mark Hanson's *The Complete Book of Alternate Tunings* has a very useful and extensive list of what artists have played in these tunings; Patrick Breen's *The Starvin' Students Alternate Tunings Workbook for Guitar* also has a very complete list. Of the other books listed, I recommend the books by Bensusan, de Grassi, and Renbourn, and 20th Century Masters books for advanced players (don't try this at home!). Chad Johnson's chord book on alternate tunings and Tom Principato's book on open string chords are simply works that contain hundreds of chord diagrams but have no explanation of how or when the chords should be used. For those who want something a little less overwhelming, Woody Mann's book is a good place to start.

List of Musical Examples on the CD*

Example 1 "Windy Blues," lowered 6th string to D
Example 2 "Up the Neck"
Example 3 "D Demon," double D tuning
Example 3a "D Demon" with strums, full version
Example 4 G tuning
Example 5 "Slidin'"
Example 6 "Slidin' #2"
Example 7 "Movin' Fast"
Example 8 "Roamin'," strum
Example 9 "Roamin'," music
Example 10 Strum
Example 11 D scale with blue notes
Example 12 "Blues without Words"
Example 13 "Lonesome Blues #2"
Example 14 "The Parlor Pedal Point Waltz"
Example 15 "Minor Claws," G minor tuning
Example 16 "Darker Than Ever"
Example 17 "The Cuckoo," melody (mountain minor tuning)
Example 18 "The Cuckoo," guitar solo
Example 19 "Dreaming," open D tuning
Example 20 "Dreaming," expanded version
Example 21 "D Blues"
Example 22 "More D Blues"
Example 23 "Ridge Runner Blues"
Example 24 "Musing"

* Recorded at Fresh Tracks, Portland, Oregon Jon Lindahl, Engineer